TACTICS
TO
WIN

T0324011

SAIL TO WIN

I would like to say a huge thank you to my lovely wife Emma for giving me the time to write this – I did try to keep it to 10 minutes an evening once the kids were asleep!

Thank you to all my excellent crews over the years who have dragged me round the course and enabled me to sail in many classes and experience lots of tactical situations on which this book is based.

Many thanks to Tim 'Sat Nav' Garvin for taking the time to read the draft of this book and provide many excellent inputs; his eye for detail is far better than mine!

TACTICS
TO
WIN

Nick Craig

FERNHURST
BOOKS

Reprinted in 2024 by Fernhurst Books Limited

Copyright © 2018 Fernhurst Books Limited
First published in 2018 by Fernhurst Books Limited

The Windmill, Mill Lane, Harbury, Leamington Spa, Warwickshire. CV33 9HP. UK
Tel: +44 (0) 1926 337488 | www.fernhurstbooks.com

A catalogue record for this book is available from the British Library
ISBN 978-1-912177-09-7

Front cover photograph © Jesus Renedo / Sailing Energy
Back cover photograph © Alistair Deaves / OKDIA

All photographs © Tom Gruitt
Except: p10: Sue Pelling; p13: Raymarine; p19: Tim Hore; p26: Alistair Deaves/OKDIA; p83: Elena Giola

Designed & illustrated by Daniel Stephen
Printed in India by Thomson Press India Ltd

NICK CRAIG

MASTER TACTICIAN

Nick Craig has won championships again and again in a wide variety of classes. This has been achieved through fantastic boatspeed and boat handling, obtained through focused practice, and a tactical awareness which is second to none.

Single-hander (no spinnaker)
OK (5 x World Champion, European Champion, 9 x National Champion)
Hadron H2 (2 x National Champion)
Finn (National Champion)
Phantom (National Champion)
D-Zero (National Champion)

Single-hander (asymmetric)
D-One (3 x World Champion, 4 x European Champion, 7 x National Champion)

Double-hander (no spinnaker)
Enterprise (3 x World Champion, 6 x National Champion)

Double-hander (symmetric spinnaker)
Merlin Rocket (2 x National Champion)

Double-hander (asymmetric)
RS400 (10 x National Champion)
B14 (2 x World Champion, European Champion, 7 x National Champion)

Team Racing
BUSA Championships (2 x Champion)

In total, so far, Nick has won 46 National championships, 6 European championships and 13 World championships and he doesn't show any sign of slowing down – 3 of these championships were won in the last year! On top of this, Nick has won the UK's 'Champion of Champions' event (The Endeavour Trophy) 6 times!

Nick was awarded the YJA Yachtsman of the Year in 2011 and the Yachts & Yachting Amateur Sailor of the Year in 2013/14.

Nick's first book, *Helming to Win,* was a totally original and unique book, developed through his amazing journey from club racer to championship winner – achieved without the benefit of a coach but through his own hard work, determination and ability to analyse the reasons for his successes and failures and learn from this. *Tactics to Win* takes this journey one stage further, focussing on specific areas of strategy and tactics. Once again it is well thought out and manages to be both thorough and succinct.

ALSO BY NICK CRAIG:

HELMING TO WIN

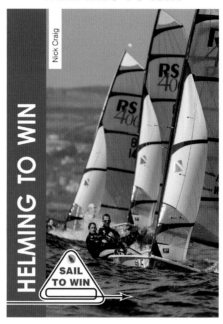

A UNIQUE ANALYSIS OF HOW TO WIN

"A welcome return of the 'Sail to Win' series from Fernhurst Books and you could hardly ask for a more qualified sailor to explain how to win races as a helm than Nick Craig."
(Yachts & Yachting, Jul 2015)

"The content is easily accessible in a very nicely managed layout that allows you to dip in for inspiration. Highly interesting, as well as hugely entertaining, to get inside the head of Nick Craig."
(OKDIA)

"Packed full of intelligent insight, brilliant top tips and engaging photo sequences."
(Sailing Magazine)

CONTENTS

FOREWORD

Boatspeed is what most sailor's concentrate on because, if you are faster than the other boats, you are going to win! However most top boats in a class go at pretty much the same speed, so sailing a shorter distance than your competitors, or in less disturbed wind or waves, are also vital ingredients to winning races. These are achieved by getting your strategy and tactics right.

In this book, multi-championship winner, Nick Craig, tells you all you need to know about strategy and tactics.

While I have enjoyed and benefitted from working with some superb coaches throughout my sailing career, Nick has not had that opportunity. He has worked it all out himself, and that makes this book especially useful. Most people reading it will, like Nick, be amateur sailors, only able to sail at weekends and the odd week for championships. To be able to learn from someone else who has trodden the same path is invaluable. He knows that you can't go sailing every day, like the Olympic sailors do, and so you have to make the most of every opportunity to learn and put into practice what you have learned.

It is so obvious from this book that this is what Nick has done. He puts every trip on the water to good use and throughout the book there are anecdotes from his sailing career. These go back to sailing Cadets in the 1980s to more recent experiences in D-Ones, OKs, Merlin Rockets and the Endeavour Trophy.

Because of Nick's amazing success in such a variety of classes he can cover tactics in single-handers, symmetric spinnaker boats and asymmetrics and you know that it is championship-winning advice in all of them!

From creating a strategy and race plan to tactics on each leg and at each mark, Nick covers it all in this excellent book. Reading it will improve your strategy and tactics and give you a better chance of winning.

Good luck!

Saskia Clark, MBE
470 sailor: 3 times Olympian: Olympic gold medallist, Rio 2016; Olympic silver medallist, London 2012; World Champion, Barcelona 2012.

CHAPTER 1

Introduction

Smart tactics are the magic ingredient which enables a fast sailor to step up from being a championship contender to a consistent championship winner. Smart tactics enable sailors to jump from boat to boat and still be in the leading group of any fleet. The joy of tactics is that they are repeatable and learnable. Boatspeed and sniffing windshifts and pressure are black arts whereas tactics can be learnt.

It is often said the highly tactical nature of sailing makes it similar to chess but on water. That is a good analogy as, just like chess, there is an exhaustive range of attacking and defensive options which can be perfected with quality practice, note taking and a keen interest in tactics. However, the analogy ends there because sailing is exhilarating, outdoor and good material for a chat over a beer after a race!

This book starts with the big picture and then drills down into starting and the race plan. It will then outline attacking and defensive options as you go through the race. Finally, this book describes boat-on-boat tactics to enable you to perform those vital close-in overtaking or defensive moves.

The best practice for tactics is racing against high quality opposition in as big a fleet as possible. I have seen teenagers come out of Youth classes with superior tactical acumen compared to the most experienced adult sailors because they have sailed in large, competitive fleets virtually every weekend whereas that fantastic experience only happens a couple of times a year in many senior classes.

> *We raced against Ben Saxton & Alan Roberts at the 2012 Endeavour Trophy and we were soundly beaten. Ben was in his early 20s at the time and I was in my late 30s having sailed the Endeavour at Burnham quite a few times. As well as being very talented, Ben & Alan had both sailed a lot of hours and, more importantly, quality hours. They both grew up sailing in large, high standard fleets so, by their early 20s, were already highly tactically astute having packed in more quality big-fleet sailing by their early 20s than most sailors manage in a lifetime.*

The young Ben Saxton & Alan Roberts win the Endearour Trophy for the first time in 2012

CHAPTER 2
Strategy

Having a big-picture strategic plan is critical before you race. From this strategy, you develop your starting and race plan and alternative plans in case things don't work out as you envisaged. Without a strategy, your start will potentially put you on the unfavoured side of the fleet and your race plan will be directionless.

Key Inputs

1. Attitude to Risk

Your attitude to risk in each race depends on whether you are ahead or behind your outcome objective. If you are ahead of your outcome objective, you should sail more conservatively. This low-risk approach typically helps deliver a consistent series. However, if you are single-mindedly focused on your outcome objective, you should increase risk to try to hit your goal if you are behind it. So you will typically start a week low risk. And hopefully end it lower risk! If you can stay low risk, others will have to increase their risk and probably rack up points. But if you're behind your objective, it may be very appropriate to hit a corner in the last race to try to claw back points to hit your goal or perhaps engage in some more aggressive, higher-risk boat-on-boat tactics.

If it is an exceptionally windy day, you may choose to reduce risk by dropping your tack rate as each tack is a potential capsize hazard. In extreme cases, this may mean starting on starboard and tacking near the left corner to enable a 2-tack beat. If you are seeking to de-risk on a windy day, you may also aim for a 1 gybe run or even tack instead of gybe ('chicken gybe').

In extreme winds, conventional wisdom says gybe when you are sailing fastest to reduce apparent wind. There are a couple of other nuances to this. Aim to gybe surfing down a wave with a big gap before the next wave and ideally on a big wave. This will give you most acceleration and time to gybe. And you should aim to gybe in a lull. Once you've found a lull and a nicely spread out wave set, that is the time to maximise speed to reduce apparent wind before the gybe.

With a leeward gate, judging the layline for the left-hand buoy (facing downwind) can be tricky but this is the buoy you are aiming to round to save on a gybe. You should bias towards overlaying as you can always drop you spinnaker early if needed and tight reach into the left-hand leeward buoy. If you underlay, you will have to gybe again to the right-hand buoy which increases risk.

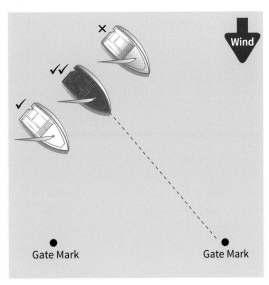

Ideally position yourself on the layline (blue) but, if not, overlay (yellow)

2. Course Bias

This is the most important factor in deciding which way you might head up the first beat. In most scenarios, you should aim to have your bow out on the long tack as soon as possible. More often than not this will lead to distance gains. So, if the first beat is starboard-tack biased, you will be looking to position your boat to the left of the fleet so that you gain from any header. As you are on starboard for most of the beat, time is on your side and at some point a header should arrive which you will profit from. You will be unlucky (or not have tracked the breeze very well) for the breeze to only shift right as you sail up the beat resulting in you losing out. Vice versa for a port-tack biased beat.

By always aiming to have your bow out on the long tack, the odds are stacked in your favour for the shifts going your way, which greatly helps deliver big fleet consistency. You should have a good reason not to have your bow out on the long tack. Even if you have no idea what the wind will do (which is more common than many sailors like to admit), following this golden rule will mean that you gain more often than not. This will make it appear that you do know what the wind is doing after all!!

Sailing can be a complex sport so when you are unsure what is happening strategically, sticking to this simple rule generally works. Awareness of how the fleet is distributed is instrumental for making this golden rule work. That is achieved through a lot of big fleet racing and being able to sail fast with your head out the boat (covered in *Helming to Win*). A top crew should have continuous awareness of your position versus the fleet and be able to feed this back as relevant.

You should keep re-assessing this and all information as you race. If the run is biased to one gybe, the beat will be biased to the other gybe, unless there is tidal influence.

" *At an OK training session at Christchurch in 2016, the run was sailed on port gybe. Everyone in the high quality training group spotted this and tacked quickly onto starboard at the leeward mark so sailing the long tack first. None of us had clocked the amount of tide we were sailing in, so the beat was actually pretty square with more breeze on the right. The first boat to tack back to the right won that mini race. So 2 lessons: 1) Allow for tide when linking run and beat course bias; 2) Something can be learnt from every race, even a short one at a training session.* "

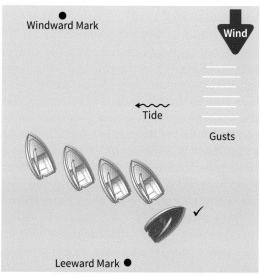

Aim to have your bow out on the long tack (blue); the two yellow boats are taking a gamble

Sometimes circumstances over-rule the general rule (e.g. more wind or a tide effect)

3. Wind Pattern

You should track the wind for as much as an hour before the start to understand the shift pattern. Typically the wind will be oscillating, swinging, bending, converging or have no pattern (rare!).

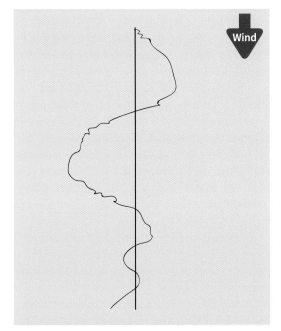

Track the wind for an hour before the start

All of these scenarios provide useful information. It is critical to be honest with yourself and not seek a pattern when there isn't one. Knowing there is no pattern is really powerful information rather than wasted time wind tracking, which may be how it feels. Knowing there is no pattern drives a strategy of sailing up the middle to hedge risk. Other sailors who have assumed a pattern may well be caught out on one side of the course by random shifts resulting in big scores for them.

You should continue to routinely track the wind between races. Practice beats can help with this.

Understanding the weather forecast to understand where the next shift may come from can help. However, weather forecasts tend to be over quite a long period and the first beat is typically short for dinghy racing. You should understand the impact of land and clouds on the breeze, whether the wind is an unstable or stable breeze, how a sea breeze may develop and its impact on the gradient wind. This is a big topic which is covered in *Wind Strategy*, also part of the Fernhurst Books' *Sail to Win* series.

The compass can play a highly effective role in helping to work out the windshift pattern before the start, ensuring that you tack on windshifts and stay in phase with shifts during the race. However, it is all too easy to become fixated with the compass and lose sight of other boats and wind patterns on the water. The compass should be glanced at occasionally, more as a support to your decision making. The compass can help you get back in phase with the windshifts if you've lost your rhythm. It can also quickly help determine if you are on a lift or header as you round the leeward mark if there isn't a land reference or you don't already have a feel for the angles.

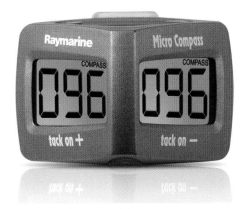

A compass can be very useful

Keep in mind that a big windshift outside of the oscillation range typically indicates a persistent shift driven by a new weather system. So, in that case, it can pay to sail into a header to find an even bigger shift and more pressure. Having your head out the boat, looking at clouds and being aware of the weather forecast help distinguish between a large oscillation and a persistent shift.

A top crew plays a key role in keeping track of the compass numbers and helping to put the helm back in phase if the helm loses rhythm.

In light winds, there is often more breeze at the edge of the course where it isn't so disturbed by the fleet. So sailing the corners more is sometimes required. Pressure is a much more important factor in light winds as a few knots more wind will make a big difference to both your speed and height whereas a few knots more wind when it is windy makes less difference.

In light winds there is more breeze at the edge

If the wind is unstable with big holes, your priorities should be more focused on sailing for pressure. If the wind is more stable, windshifts become more important than pressure differences.

A great example of this is the Ora and Peler winds at Lake Garda. The Ora in the afternoon is windy, pretty stable and with big wind bends / more pressure near the cliffs. The morning Peler thermal wind is lighter and shiftier, especially as it dies later in the morning. Very different tactical approaches are required in the morning versus the afternoon at Garda!

Standing up can provide a better view of pressure differentials over the race course, especially in light winds. These can be subtle. So, if you're not sure where there is more wind, just go with where your instincts say there is more. The more time you spend looking for breeze differences in light winds, the more often those instincts are right!

4. Tide

Prior knowledge of a venue, either through your own experience or by talking to others, is the most valuable information you can find. Tidal charts are also useful but may not be subtle or detailed enough to provide the insights you need for short-course dinghy sailing.

You can often find information on the day by observing where shallow water may be, looking for tide lines and seeing who gains in split tacks with a tuning partner. On your practice beat, you should stop next to any buoys or fixed points up the course to see how much tide there is and whether that varies over the course.

During the race, you should keep your head out of the boat and observe any tide differences. The best indicator is whether boats are gaining from different parts of the course that doesn't seem to be related to wind differences.

After each race, you should go over the race again in your mind to try to work out which way is paying to work out where shallow and deep water might be.

A top crew can play a key role in tracking the fleet and helping to determine which way is paying. Having a handle on this during the race is very helpful to modify your game plan if necessary.

5. Land Influence

It is rare that land doesn't have a major influence on the wind on dinghy racing courses. Many books have been written about this so justice couldn't be done on this subject here!

As well as the impact of land on wind bends and convergence, you should consider how stable the wind is. For example, offshore winds tend to be more unstable which moves your strategy towards taking shifts up the middle of the course.

A buddy boat can help with understanding if there are biases in the beat created by tide or wind patterns. A buddy boat should ideally be of similar speed to you. You can take split tacks and explore different parts of the beat to understand which way is paying.

6. Waves

There are sometimes significantly bigger waves or choppier water on one part of the course, which may lead you to avoid that part of the beat especially in a skiff where chop can prevent upwind planing. Choppy water may also indicate shallow water or a tide line which may be useful information for your tidal strategy.

7. Length of Beat / Size of Fleet

In a big fleet with a short first beat, going right can pay handsomely if all other things are equal. Going left means quickly being boxed in over the port layline and unable to cross starboard tack boats. You need to be at least a boat length ahead to cross a starboard tacker when on port which may be hard to make on a short beat.

This is a rare scenario as first beats are generally a decent length in big fleets but, with courses generally shrinking, this situation does arise.

> ❝ *At the 2016 Merlin Rocket Nationals practice race, a short first beat and starboard-biased start line was set. Everyone rounding the first windward mark in the top 10 started at or near the starboard end of the line. Without a big left windshift, there was no way back from a mid or port end start even with a great start and boatspeed.* ❞

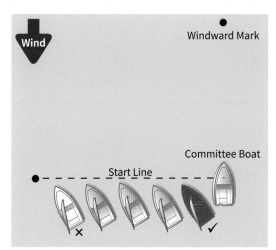

With a starboard biased line and a short first beat you need to start near the starboard end of the line (blue)

The Plan

Based on these 7 factors, you should form an idea of which way you think will pay up the beat. It is critical to be honest with yourself. Being not sure is absolutely fine and pretty common. That in itself is a good thing as you can then manage risk effectively and stick to the middle of the fleet. Only taking a side of the fleet when you are very sure, and sailing around the middle when you're not, is one of the magic ingredients of the holy grail of big fleet consistency.

You should talk to people who have sailed at your venue before the event to see if they have any insights, use any information available online and dig into your venue notes – you should keep a record of what works at different venues for future reference.

This can seem complex. In the heat of a big-fleet event, it often pays not to overthink and go with your instincts. Those instincts are formed from all your years of sailing condensed into a split second decision (isn't the human brain amazing!) so use them and develop them through as much big-fleet sailing as possible.

Risk Management

You should have a clear outcome objective for your event before you go into it. However, at the event, you should focus on process objectives rather than your outcome objective because the outcome of the event is not in your control. So focusing on outcome goals at an event can lead to frustration and a worse performance. You can sail a brilliant week but not win if someone else is on absolute fire. Your goals should be focused on what you can control – for example, sailing the right course, not forgetting anything each day (such as tallies). You can't control whether you hit the groove of the waves and shifts that week or how well your opposition sails.

So coming 50th at an event can be a great result if you've hit all your process objectives, whereas you might not be wholly happy if you've missed your process objectives but won.

This approach is a great way to de-pressure and de-stress events.

Having said all that, half of your brain still needs to be focused on your outcome objective so that you can effectively manage risk. This is a hard mental exercise to pull off which becomes easier with more experience of sailing in high quality, big fleets.

If you are behind your outcome objective, you should increase risk. That means more punchy starts, sailing harder to the side of the course that you think may pay, pushing your boat handling harder and edging towards more 50/50 situations in boat-on-boat rules situations.

If you are ahead of your outcome objective, you should be more conservative. However, backing down too much on starts will lead to a poor start. So, if you are de-risking, it generally works to still start pretty hard but stay with the fleet strategically, be highly conservative with the rules and take some more time on boat handling, especially if it is windy.

> *It is good to have an idea where you are versus your outcome objective even before an event starts. We went into the 2008 Endeavour Trophy with a very light wind forecast and we were a few stone heavier than some of the potential contenders. Our outcome objective was to win. We knew that if we started reasonably well, we might just make the top 5. So we aimed to win every start by pushing the line and starting right at the end of the biased start lines to take every inch of line bias. The strategy carried a high risk of multiple OCSs in an 8 race, 1 discard series. But it gave us a crack at winning; we were solely focused on that outcome objective. We just got away with the starts and won overall.*

Sailing the Fleet

Managing risk is about where you are positioned relative to the fleet not where you are versus the course. So you could be in the middle of the course but if most of the fleet is one side of you, you are taking a big risk (which may or may not be appropriate in that race). You should always have

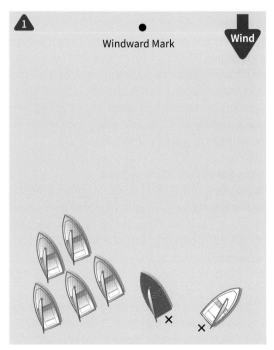

Yellow & blue are near the middle of the course, but not the fleet and are therefore taking a risk

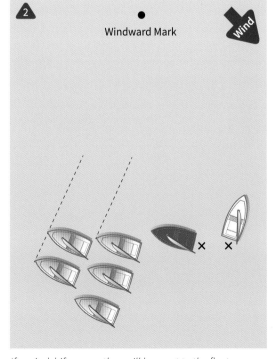

If a windshift comes they will lose out to the fleet

an idea where you are versus the fleet. This is a key role of a top crew.

With plenty of big fleet experience, where you are relative to the fleet becomes instinctive so you can spend minimal time looking at this and focus on boatspeed and windshifts. With a drilled-in risk-averse approach, you should feel uncomfortable as soon as you start splitting from the fleet so be looking for the first shift / gust to get back across to the fleet to consolidate, unless your clear plan for that race is to gamble.

Keeping to the middle of the fleet is easier upwind than downwind. Clear wind and waves are critical downwind but they are rarely found in the middle of the pack. If you are seeking to sail the fleet downwind, you should still aim to cover the middle of the fleet if possible but be very aware of being caught in dirty wind and waves.

Downwind, you should be more prepared to split from the fleet to find clear wind and water because sailing in the middle of the fleet downwind may be conservative but it can be just slow. Of course, if you can find clear wind and water in middle of the fleet, that is ideal!

Ideally downwind you would be in the middle of the fleet in clear air (like blue)

You want to avoid being in the middle of the fleet in dirty air (like yellow)

Although you may still be able to find a narrow lane in the middle of the fleet

CHAPTER 3

Starting

Being able to start consistently well in big fleets is a key skill for delivering a consistent series.

Starting is a process, albeit a relatively complex one. Like any process it can be perfected if each part of it is well practised. So it is easier to perfect starting than picking shifts or sailing fast downwind, which are more of an art rather than a process.

Conversely, starts are less important in smaller fleets and shiftier winds so the ability to start consistently well is a key factor in the transition from a leading club racer to championship contender.

Slow Speed Boat Handling

Slow speed boat handling is the foundation for strong starting. It is a distinct skill; sailors can be fantastic at normal speed boat handling and many aspects of the sport but still weak at slow speed boat handling. However, it is an area few sailors practise.

Boats behave very differently at fast and slow speeds. At slow speeds, the foils start to stall or are completely stalling so that your boat becomes a very different and tricky beast. So practising controlling your boat at slow speeds is key to starting consistently well.

Being able to handle your boat effectively at slow speeds will enable you to generate space quickly on a start line, thus reducing the time available for anyone else to fill that critical space.

Stalling Foils

As your boat slows, the flow over your foils will eventually stall. Your boat then behaves totally differently.

Starting well is hard because everyone is sailing slowly with potentially stalling foils and boats which are difficult to handle. This is how start line pile-ups arise!

The key is to practise sailing your boat with both stalled foils and foils on the edge of stalling. You need to learn where that knife-edge of stalling foils is for your boat in all conditions.

You should aim to be able to stay on that knife-edge of stalling foils more effectively than your competition. By doing that, you can crucially creep towards the line more slowly than other boats in the last minute before the start and in control. This gives you more space to accelerate and more options.

You should also practise generating a gap to leeward as quickly as possible. This is achieved by being able to sail your boat up to head to wind and even slightly beyond head to wind, without losing control. While you have no rights if you point beyond head to wind, you can briefly do this to gain more space to leeward so long as you don't infringe other boats. So being able to steer some big angles and manage that with aggressive but legal rudder use, heel and sail trim is a key skill. The precise combination of these three weapons (rudder, heel and sail trim) that is most effective varies by boat but can be learnt with practice.

In general, leeward heel will help keep your foils biting longer. In lighter winds, this generally means standing up rather than sitting comfortably on the sidedeck digesting your breakfast!

You should practise controlling your boat with stalled foils. So then, if you do slow down to the point that your foils stall, by accident or design, you can remain in control.

Exercises

An effective exercise for learning about your boat's stalling foils is to stop by a mark and aim to stay within around a boat's length of it for two minutes. You should vary that boat-length gap depending on how easy your boat is to handle at low speeds, the wind strength and how experienced you are at this.

As part of that exercise, you should aim to be at as near to full speed as you can by the mark on the 'start gun'. Being able to bring your boat up to speed, known as 'pulling the trigger', in as short a space of time and distance as possible is a critical skill in a crowded start.

This isn't the most exciting exercise, so trying this little but often works well to stave off boredom. Do this two or three times before racing every time you sail and you will quickly develop great slow-speed boat handling skills.

You should line up next to the buoy at different angles to simulate both a starboard and port-biased start line.

The Start Process

1 Hour to 10 Minutes Pre-start

This is a key time because your information gathering during this period will determine your chances of getting the first beat right.

However, it is absolutely OK, and pretty common, not to know which way will pay up the first beat. Be honest with yourself about this because a rash decision that one way is favoured means that you will be taking uncalculated risks which typically means the points will rack up over a week.

If you are unsure, sail up the middle of the course relative to the fleet.

Your starting strategy is closely linked to your first beat plan so this information is doubly important.

The table overleaf shows the 9 different start scenarios depending on the line and first beat bias. This should help you to develop your starting strategy.

Practise staying by a mark for 2 minutes

	Start line bias	Pre-race analysis	Starting strategy
1	Starboard	Go right	Start on, or very near to, the committee boat so you can tack early and get your bow out on the tack towards the favoured side. This is a high risk start so should be considered in the context of your risk management for that race. Only a few boats will pull this start off. Most boats will find themselves in the second row or caught on the wrong side of the committee boat or, worse, infringing the committee boat and doing a 720^0 penalty. If you are planning on starting next to the committee boat, consider the impact of a wind shadow next to a large committee boat. You may choose to start a few lengths down to avoid that shadow and gain a jump on those starting right next to the boat. This should still allow an early tack out to the favoured side.
2	Starboard	Go up the middle	Start near the committee boat to take advantage of the bias but look for space and aim to quickly drive over the fleet on starboard tack to get into the middle of the course.
3	Starboard	Go left	Similar to start 2 but space to leeward out the start is everything as you will have to live with the lane you create out the start for some time.
4	Unbiased	Go right	Depending on how strongly you think right will pay, and your attitude to risk for that race, start towards, or even right next to, the committee boat to enable an early tack to the right hand side. It can even pay to start in the second row, but right next to the committee boat, at speed with room to tack.
5	Unbiased	Go up the middle	Start around the middle of the fleet (not necessarily the middle of the line) in as much space as you can to give early room to tack, providing flexibility for your route decisions.
6	Unbiased	Go left	Depending on how strongly you think left will pay, and your attitude to risk for that race, you should be starting towards, or even next to, the pin end.
7	Port	Go right	Start towards the pin end to take advantage of the line bias. Seek to create a gap in front / leeward of yourself in the pre-start and use up all of leeward gap in the last seconds before the start to create room to tack early.
8	Port	Go up the middle	Same as start 7 as you are also looking for an early tack out in this scenario.
9	Port	Go left	Start near, or even on, the pin end. A gap to leeward is key as you will have to live with the lane you create out the start for some time. Starting right on the pin is high risk but guarantees a great lane, with no-one to leeward of you, if you pull off a winning pin end start.

> At the 2015 Endeavour Trophy, the race officer had smartly set a port-biased line as right was the paying way as it was in shallow water so avoiding the adverse tide. A port-biased line prevents a committee boat pile up but makes for a competitor dilemma. Do you take advantage of the port line bias and risk being hung out to dry in the tide if there is no room to tack, or start on the committee boat to escape the tide but lose line bias? The best start is one near the port end where you can tack onto port straight away. We pulled this off but unfortunately Ben Saxton & Toby Lewis did this slightly better and rolled us as we headed to shore securing yet another race win for them!

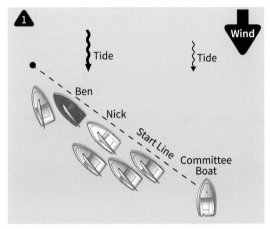

We wanted to benefit from the port line bias, but be able to tack into less tide

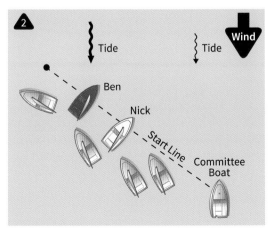

Unfortunately Ben pulled it off better than us!

You should overlay your attitude to risk for that race on your starting strategy, backing away from the ends or crowds if you are looking for a low-risk race. Starting at the ends is especially high risk because, if it all goes wrong, you may hit the committee boat or pin end or miss the line, whereas the cost of a poor start away from the ends is usually less.

You should also know your boat and your capability in it. Some boats are harder to handle in tight situations (e.g. skiffs). Quality pre-start boat handling requires practice. So if you are new to a boat, or rusty, you may back-off from tight spots at main events (but not training events!). If you are well practised in the boat you are sailing, you can be punchier with your starting plan.

In very light winds, it often pays to start at the ends, especially in big fleets. The wind has little energy so dirty air and the deflection of wind as it passes over the fleet is bigger, making the ends better places to start.

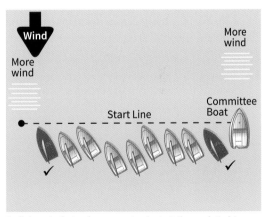

In light winds, it often pays to start at the ends in big fleets

You need to practise all these types of starts in your training events so you become 100% comfortable with every type of start in all situations (light winds, windy, tidal etc.). This is a key set of skills to enable big-fleet consistency so you can deliver great starts in all situations rather than the occasional great start and then weaker starts in your unfavoured scenarios which lead to inconsistent results.

You will know which of these starting types you relish and which you approach with slight trepidation. You should put yourself out of your comfort zone at training events, challenging yourself to pull off great starts in your weaker areas. Also start in the pack at training events to improve your ability to pull off the really tough starts. It is rare that there is lots of space in a big fleet start so, by pushing yourself to start in the pack at smaller events, you can simulate big fleet starts all year round rather than just a few times a year. This will accelerate your learning curve massively.

10 Minutes to 5 Minutes Pre-start

Once you have gathered all your information about the race track for the day, it is time to check transits and line bias. Whilst doing this, you should remain aware of anything that may change your first beat plan, especially the windshift and gust pattern. So keep your head out of the boat and looking up the race course while performing these transits and line bias checks.

It is rare that there is a perfect transit on the shore in line with the start line. If there isn't, this should not be a concern. You should aim to have two or three transits at either end of the line: ideally, one for when you are over the line, one on and one behind the line. And, if you can, develop a picture of what you see in between them. This typically means having a look down the line several times so that you can form a map of the start line geography in your head, at both ends if possible. In the reality of the last seconds before the start on a crowded start line, it is rare that you will find you're on a line transit, but just a glimpse of what you can recall on the landscape can give you the confidence to take a crucial jump on the fleet.

If there are no transits this is, in many ways, a great opportunity for a flying start! No one else will have a transit so there is typically a lot of line sag. This presents the chance to make a jump on the fleet away from the ends if that fits with your first beat plan.

There is typically more line sag on longer start lines, lower quality fleets and where there is more adverse tide and wind or waves. So be comfortable taking a jump on the fleet if those factors are in play.

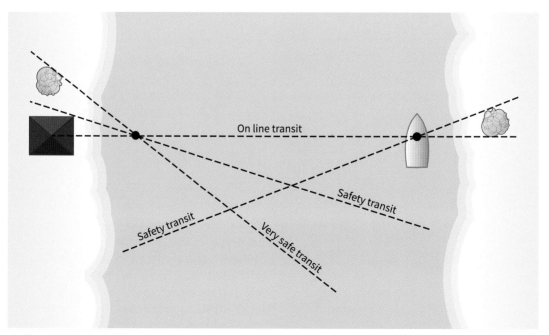

Getting transits

5 Minutes to 1 Minute (or sooner depending on the boat) Pre-start

During this period, you should still very much keep your head out of the boat and be aware of any changes in the wind across the course or signs of change from the clouds. Consider the impact of any changes on your starting plans both in terms of line bias and which way may pay up the first beat.

As you move towards a minute (or sooner with a densely-populated start line), you should find space in the area that you would like to start. You should remain flexible. For example, if the line is starboard biased but you want a low-risk start, this generally means starting away from the committee boat. However, if everyone is doing that, there is sometimes lots of room at the committee boat. That often happens early in a series when most boats are looking to de-risk their starts.

Starting in as much space as possible reduces the damage of a sub-standard start. With fewer boats around you, there is much more likely to be room to tack or sail free and find a lane than if you are starting in a pack.

Choosing who you line up near is very important. Ideally you should line up near boats that you know you can outpace. However, you should avoid lining up next to someone who might be out of control. Whilst an out-of-control boat may be penalised with a 720^0 penalty, an incident just before the start can ruin your start no matter how much in the right you are!

Starting next to an in-control, but slower, boat gives you a strong chance of gaining a crucial early lane and also starting worry free. By the same token, it is very powerful to gain a reputation for being fast and difficult to start near (so others avoid starting near you). This is worth cultivating at training events.

The Final Minute Pre-start

You should be seeking to line up bow down of the boats around you i.e. further back from the start line than the other boats with your bow just overlapped with the front row to keep your

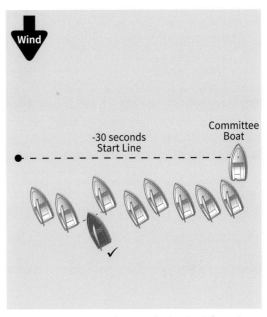

Ideally position yourself slightly further back from the boats around you with 30 seconds to go

'starting slot'.

By lining up down versus other boats, you are highly unlikely to be black flagged or put your sail number in the race officer's head. Lining up bow down also means that you have more space to accelerate into before hitting the start line than the boats around you. So you can sheet in before everyone else and hit the start line with more speed. Also, lining up bow down means that you don't reveal where your transits are.

On a port-biased line, when you sheet in on starboard you make less distance towards the line than on a starboard-biased line. So you can typically sheet in earlier on a port-biased start line.

You should reveal your transit as late as possible. So, ideally, you should sheet in and accelerate once and not have to slow down again, whilst using up every inch of your transit. Not easy! Judging time and distance is key for this. Spending some time pre-start understanding your speed of travel versus your transits can be a helpful exercise, especially in tide.

Lining up bow down is potentially a risky starting strategy because if you don't sheet in before the boats around you, they will roll you.

The key to making this work is confidence in your transits and the time and distance it takes to reach those transits. If you are 100% confident in both, anyone who sheets in before you will be OCS so it is unlikely that anyone will do that. If you are not fully confident in your transits or time and distance to the start line, you should de-risk by lining up further forward on the boats around you.

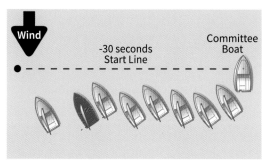

If you aren't 100% confident in your transits, line up further forward

You should create space to leeward as late as possible to reduce the risk of the lovely gap that you have hopefully created being filled by a latecomer. Being able to create that gap quickly is a key benefit of practising your slow-speed boat handling.

With a **starboard-biased start** line, you are looking for a gap to leeward as it is going to take some time to get your bow forward on your opposition so that you have enough room to tack. You are going to have to live with the lane you created pre-start for some time, so a gap to leeward is important.

In lighter winds, you should aim to create a bigger gap to leeward as acceleration from near stationary to full speed takes longer.

In the last minute, you need to be highly aware of boats potentially coming in and filling your gap to leeward. In a 2-man boat, the helm should be more visually focused to leeward as a fast reaction is needed to stop a boat filling your gap to leeward. The crew should then be more focused on looking to windward for transits and cover.

To prevent someone filling your lovely leeward gap, you need to temporarily fill the gap before they arrive. This will generally deter the gap filler and they will sail along the line and seek an easier gap. You should fill the gap by bearing off hard so that your boat spins 90° which fills the gap more effectively. You should bear off 'badly' such that you move forward as little as possible so not losing too much of your gap to leeward. A bad bear off uses lots of rudder to slow you down. To do this, use heel and sail trim to fight the turn so you need to use more rudder to turn (i.e. leeward heel and main sheeted in and jib eased as you bear off). As soon as the boat potentially filling your gap has headed on their way, you should luff back up hard and use the momentum from your bear off to claw back some distance to windward so re-creating your gap to leeward. All of these moves are difficult and need practice in training time.

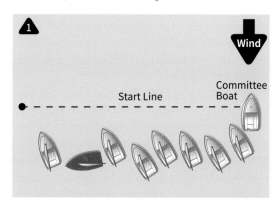

To protect your leeward gap, bear away sharply

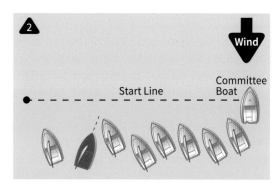

And then luff hard to claw back some distance to windward

If you find yourself in a pile-up, or even just a crowd, from which a good start looks challenging, be quick to escape and find space if you see there is more space elsewhere.

With a **port-biased start line**, you are generally looking to tack early to consolidate a hopefully strong start. To do this, a gap to windward is needed. So create a gap to leeward in the pre-start period and then sheet in really early to use up that gap and create a gap to windward on the starting signal. This gives you the room to tack early. If you don't envisage that you will be able to tack quickly, you also need to leave some gap to leeward so you can maintain a lane out the start. This is a very hard start to pull off, but potentially very rewarding as not many boats will manage it. If you can make room to be one of the first to tack out, you are probably laughing your way to at least a top 5 placing at the windward mark!

You should review how often you are OCS. If this is rare, especially at training events, you should be pushing your starts harder.

As you accelerate for the start, in order to ideally hit the line at full speed on the start gun, ensure that you use heel and sail trim to accelerate. This will maximise acceleration and hopefully give an edge on the boats around you. Your bear off to accelerate should be initiated with windward heel and early jib trim. You should then straighten your course and then luff with leeward heel and fast main trimming.

There is a lot going on during this last minute but you also need to keep your head out of the boat and stay observant, especially in shifty unstable breezes. You may need to change your plan quickly and move up or down the line if you see new pressure or a shift coming. This is a key role of a top crew.

The First Minute Post-start

Gains in the first minute of the race are massively magnified as you move through the race as the early leaders benefit from clear air, clear water and control of their race plan. So hiking at your absolute hardest as soon as there is wind on for at least the first minute, or until you poke your bow out from the pack, is very rewarding. Sprint hiking and trimming hard for 10 seconds can work to nudge your nose out. Sprint hiking is when you hike to your absolute maximum for a burst and then rest up a little to let the blood flow back through your legs. In light winds, all the smooth steering and movement you have practised (see *Helming to Win*) should give you the confidence to relax and sail fast.

In this first minute, you should drive home your first beat strategy:

- If your plan is to go left then, if there is space, sail a little lower on starboard than usual.
- If you are unsure which way will pay and find you are to the left of the fleet, sail a bit higher or tack on the next small shift or gap.
- If you are looking to head right, you should tack early or proactively find a lane to tack by sailing high to force the boats above you to tack, or if your start was not so good, look for a gap to tack and duck transoms.

You should sail high or low using your rig set-up and heel rather than pulling on your rudder too much:

- To sail high: a touch of leeward heel, more sheet tension and kicker, draft back on sails. Consistency of heel maintains flow over your foils so, if you do need to sail with heel, aim to keep the amount of heel stable. Leeward heel adds bite to your foils so you are less likely to slip sideways which can be very helpful – for example, if you are trying to live in a leebow situation where you might be pinching and therefore slowed, giving an increased risk of slipping sideways.
- To sail low: dead flat, more forgiving leeches and draft forward.

You should weigh up making these potential adjustments versus the distance lost whilst making them. Adjusting heel and sheet tension is easy and generally loses no distance. Adjusting kicker and draft may take more time and lose distance if you have to move in from hiking or lose precision of steering to make the adjustments. You should work on being able to make adjustments with minimal distance loss. A top crew can make these adjustments whilst the helm keeps their head out of the boat and in rhythm with the windshifts – Alan Roberts is outstanding at this in a Merlin.

You should always stay positive about a poor start line as they present a great opportunity! A biased, short and congested start line means that only a few boats will get a decent start. Make sure you are one of them!

> ❝ *I wasn't at the 2016 OK Worlds but I heard lot of stories and moans about how poor the start lines were. They were biased and congested in unstable wind. The one person I spoke to who didn't complain was Jim Hunt who is an excellent starter. He took the opportunity these start lines presented, won the starts and the week with a race to spare!* ❞

Jim Hunt, an excellent starter, sailing an OK

Recovery from Poor Starts

Unless you are a starting god, your starts will occasionally go wrong. So the ultimate big fleet sailing weapon is being able to recover from a poor start or first shift. This is another key ingredient in the holy grail of big-fleet consistency.

Revisit Strategy

With everything happening fast, it is often time trust your instincts. Instincts are developed from past experiences so are often right in the heat of the battle when you have little time to rethink your plan. If you have time, get your head out of the boat and look for any factors that may change your strategy.

Clean Air

If you have a poor start you may be a couple of lengths behind the leaders at that point. If you can arrive at the windward mark still only a couple of lengths behind the leaders, you will certainly be in the top five! The key reasons for bigger losses than the couple of initial boat lengths lost from a poor start is sailing in dirty air and off strategy.

Dirty air is a killer because the wind is slowed but, more importantly, confused. That confused air makes it nearly impossible to set up your rig to work efficiently. So it is very challenging to stay in the groove resulting in a loss of both speed and height, a horrible combination!

The most dirty air and water is at the start because the fleet is at its most compact. Finding clear wind is challenging in a big fleet after a poor start. So you should look for reasonable lanes of clear wind whilst still going the right way according to your first beat game plan (or revised plan if you have seen something change).

If you are forced to sail in dirty air, adapt your dynamic settings so your rig copes more effectively with wind that is confused in direction and strength. You should use less mainsheet and kicker tension allowing your sails to breathe more easily and provide more acceleration as dirty air slows you up.

Holding Lanes

Knowing what a 'lane' of clear air looks like for your class of boat and your sailing style is critical. Some boats can sail well in a leebow position, others can't. Where the dirty wind sits to leeward of another boat's sails varies by type of boat. Understanding these two things is key to understanding where the lanes may be for your boat.

Two-boat tuning and putting yourself under pressure at training events is a great way of learning how to sail effectively in 'narrow lanes' vs. 'fat lanes'. In two-boat tuning, you should practise sailing in difficult positions. That will narrow the lanes you are able to hold. The narrower lane you can still sail reasonably fast in will dramatically improve your chances of finding a lane that keeps you on your first beat game plan. This is the main reason why some sailors can recover from a poor start better than others. They can live in a narrow lane and so spend less time being bounced from tack to tack letting them get back on their race plan quickly.

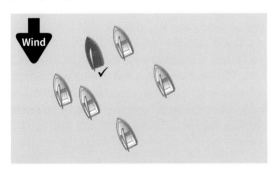

Blue has a clear lane with undisturbed air

Yellow is stuck in dirty air and doesn't have a clear lane

Blue has a clear lane, but is taking a risk by being one side of the fleet

Depending on how the class takes being leebowed, yellow may have a lane, but may not

Two-boat tuning in tight spots will enable you to recognise immediately when you are in an irrecoverable leebow position or cover whilst racing. This speeds up your decision making so you spend less time in bad positions!

You can sail for longer in a tight spot using your settings and heel. So, if you are in danger of being leebowed, move into 'high' mode with tighter leeches, a touch of leeward heel and sail draft back. Do the opposite to sail free if you are in danger of being rolled to windward. You should also use these techniques to expand your lanes to ensure they are more sustainable.

Lanes are more important in steady wind and on one-sided courses as you will have to live with the lane you pick, and then try to expand, for longer. In very shifty winds, finding a lane doesn't really matter as your next tack isn't far away. So finding, expanding and keeping lanes are key skills in the transition from a good lake sailor to a top-drawer sea / big fleet sailor.

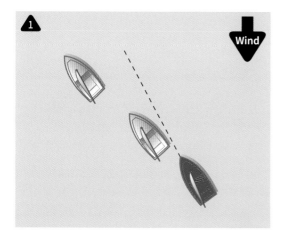

Sailing high to expand your lane

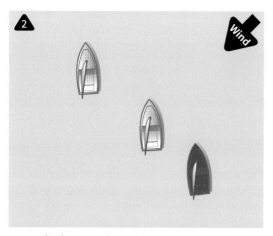

No need to lose speed expanding lane, because the windshift has achieved that

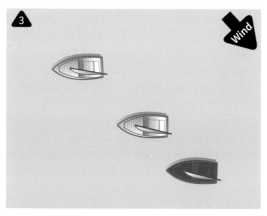

This windshift means that lots of lane expansion is needed… or time to tack!

In addition, anticipating the next shift will help you know in which direction your lane needs to be expanded. If you are expecting a header and have a boat underneath you, the header could make that boat become a leebow boat. If you are going to tack anyway on the header and you have room to do so, there is no issue. If you would like to sail on through the header (for example, anticipating a bigger header, to sail to better tide etc.), then it may be worth sailing high to create space away from the potential leebow position that the upcoming header may deliver.

Chip Away v. Corners

In general, it pays to chip places away after a poor start by finding lanes to the favoured side of the race course. However, hitting a corner usually delivers clean air so is often a better plan than sailing in the middle of the pack with dirty wind and confused water. So, if you can't find any lanes, corners are preferable. Being able to sail in a narrow lane opens up tactical options and helps you avoid high risk corners.

Hitting a corner is high risk as even a small shift can lose you a lot of places especially on a big course. Or gain them! So in some circumstances a corner is appropriate: for example, if you need a top five position in the last race of an event to achieve your outcome objective and chipping away is unlikely to get you there from a mid-fleet position, hitting a corner is a very appropriate plan.

Handicap Racing Starts

If you are starting in a mixed fleet and you are sailing a relatively slow boat, it typically pays to start at the ends especially for a starboard-biased line. This helps prevent you being sailed over by faster boats too early in the race and gives you a quick route to clean air if you need it by tacking onto port. If you are in a slow boat, you are probably going to need to sail to the edges of the course because the fast boats will be ahead and so have churned up the wind and water across most of the course.

On a port-biased line, in a fast boat, winning the end is very powerful as you can use your speed straight away without being impeded by slower, higher pointing boats. If you are a slow boat, the pin end only works if you can get your bow out sufficiently to squeeze out faster boats and stop them rolling you. More likely to work is a start away from the end with room to tack so you can quickly find clear wind away from the fast boats.

If you are starting in a fast boat, you have more flexibility on where to start. However, fast boats tend to point lower than slower boats so you may need a wider starting lane than other boats, which is usually found away from the busier ends of the line.

Gate Starts

When to Start

When you start should be assessed against the distribution of the fleet and not distance along the gate. So a start 2 minutes into a 4 minute gate is early if most of the fleet start late and vice versa.

A good conservative strategy is to start towards the middle of the pack, but in space.

More boats are able to execute a good start on a gate start whereas this is harder to achieve on a line start. So it generally takes longer to find space to tack after a gate start because more boats have good starts. As you are forced stay on starboard out the line for longer by more good starters, any leverage versus the fleet at the start is magnified. So starting to one side of the fleet is higher risk than on a line start. That risk can be appropriate depending on where you are versus your objectives and how confident you are about which way will pay.

If you are slower than the fleet in the conditions of the day, consider starting late. If you start early and are slow you are likely to be spat out of the back of the fleet and have to sail in horrible dirty air and water for longer. If you are fast, an early start would seem logical but remains high risk. It is rare that a boat has such a significant speed

advantage versus the fleet that they can create space for an early tack. So an early start usually results in heading pretty hard left up the beat which is high risk.

If you are planning on starting late, ensure that you very precisely watch the time passed after the start. Give yourself at least 15 seconds of leeway versus the gate closing time. This approach avoids taking an unnecessary risk of the gate closing or a late starter pile up. But stay aware – if everyone follows this advice there could be perfect clear wind and water available by pushing the start a little later!

Where to Sit Pre-start

In the pre-start period, you should sit just above the gate boat's layline. A typical routine is to beat from the start buoy with around 3 minutes to go until the start. Stop about half way along the gate e.g. 2 minutes for a 4 minute gate. Then sit just above the pathfinder's course on port from the start buoy. This ensures that you won't get caught out late if the wind lifts on port.

As the start gets nearer, you should track back to just below the expected course of the pathfinder but stay highly aware of any windshifts or changes in direction of the pathfinder, especially in unstable breeze. If you are unsure whether you are high or low of the gate, sheet in upwind on starboard and look at the bow of the gate boat. If you are gaining land or horizon compared to the gate boat, you are crossing ahead. If you are losing land or horizon compared to it, keep sailing fast because you are late!! This is also a useful trick for knowing where you are compared to the fleet or if you are crossing a particular boat at any point on the race course.

You should continue to track the breeze. If you find yourself headed on starboard, you should consider moving up the line to take advantage of the subsequent lift back (assuming an oscillating breeze rather than a persistent shift). And consider heading down the line and starting earlier if you find yourself lifted on starboard in an oscillating breeze.

Also in patchy wind, starting in a lull is a

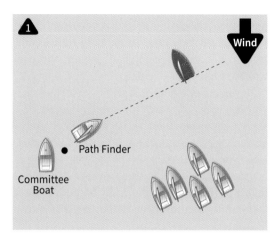

Sit just above the gate boat's layline

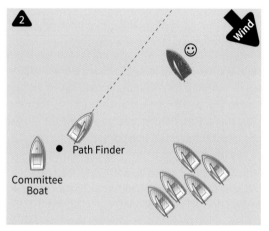

If the wind swings to port you will still be OK

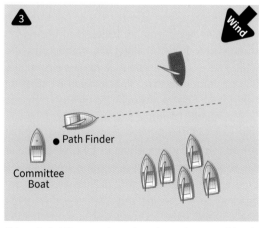

If the wind shifts to starboard you have time to sail back behind the line

nightmare as you will find the boats starting before you able to cross you and you will also potentially be rolled by the boats above you. With patchy wind, it is critical to try to start in pressure, but not easy! So be prepared to move down or up the line to start in pressure. Ensure that you have your head out of the boat in these conditions, looking at what pressure is coming down the race course. Standing up gives a better view of this, especially in a crowded fleet.

Just as for a line start, you should be working a gap to leeward in the last minute before the start. As you approach the start, you should seek to slow up the boats to windward to increase your gap to leeward whilst being mindful that no-one ducks your stern and takes your leeward gap. You should aim to keep the boats to windward of you overlapped to prevent that happening. You need to be careful how aggressively you pursue this as you can win the battle but not the war! You can do a great job of holding the pack up above you but, if you cause a pile-up, you may well become entangled in the mess. You will be in the right but that won't help your start and there is no redress for someone infringing you (unless there is serious damage). The offending boat or boats may do their 720^0 penalties but you've still got a lousy start!

Again earning a reputation for being a tough starter at training events is a sound investment as people will seek to start nearer slower, easier boats to start with. This creates space for punchier starters.

The Start
If you have created space to leeward, you should ideally approach the gate on a close reach. You should cross the stern of the gate boat closely (how close depends on your attitude to risk in that race) and use heel and sail trim to luff to a close hauled course as you round the gate so avoiding use of the rudder (handbrake). If you can, you should give an early squeeze to windward to create a gap to windward by leebowing the boats above you to allow early room to tack. Sometimes you can catch the stern wave of the gate boat to gain a kick to

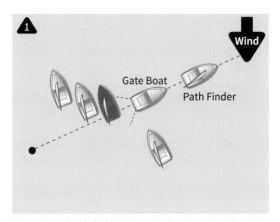

Rounding closely behind the gate boat and catching the stern wave can give you a kick to windward

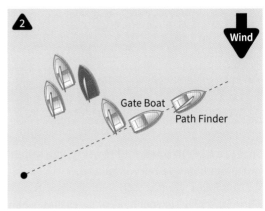

Which may leave you in a position to tack out early

windward. It is often the boats who are able to tack early out the gate and start working the shifts who are the leaders to the windward mark.

After the Start

There is a lot more leverage on a gate than a line start. A gate is also typically longer than a line start and more people have the opportunity to get a good start.

So, if you start well, it is important to consolidate early by tacking across the fleet on the first small shift if you are to the left of the pack or drive low and fast if you are to the right of the pack. This does depend on your first beat strategy though.

Remember, if there isn't room to tack you can still reduce exposure to late starters by using the techniques described earlier.

A gate start

CHAPTER 4

The Race Plan

Once you have decided your strategy, you should formulate a race plan and a few alternative plans in case other boats de-rail your plan A.

This helps greatly with your mental rehearsal of the race. Playing through your plan A and alternative plans in your head ensures that, when you race for real, there are few surprises. By avoiding surprises, you can calmly execute your manoeuvres without feeling pressure.

First Beat Plan

You should have a plan of where you are going to start and your planned tacks towards the windward mark. Of course, it is rare that this plan exactly transpires as the wind is constantly changing in strength and direction, which changes your plan. But it is good to have a broad idea of where you want to go. This way, you will be more in control and less likely to be forced into incorrect route decisions by other boats. By knowing your plan, you will duck a stern when needed or not duck and seek to tack and leebow a boat when that works for your race plan.

Having no plan typically results in a race spent sailing around in dirty air in the pack being bounced from tack to tack by other boats. Know that horrible feeling?!

Tack Rate

As you form your race plan, you should assess your tack rate for the day. That depends on the class of boat you're racing, wind strength and wave state. Your tack rate is governed by how effectively you can tack in the conditions of the day. Different types of boat lose more distance on tacks than others. So tacking a Firefly or Enterprise in light winds loses very little distance whereas tacking a skiff, catamaran or yacht loses a lot more distance.

If the first beat is short, you should consider a low-tack strategy, especially if the wind is steady.

Some distance is lost on every tack and, on a short first beat, a boat length can be the difference between rounding in the lead versus out the top 5.

Improving your boat handling (covered in *Helming to Win*) will raise your effective tack rate which opens up a wider range of tactical options. You can also use your high and low pointing grooves to reduce your tack rate if that is appropriate.

> At the 2017 Australian B14 Nationals, we had a reasonable start in the opening race and tacked onto port after about a minute on a big shift. We tacked again a minute or so later on another big shift but were surprised to find ourselves back in 10th after two good shifts. The leaders had tacked less than us and sailed into more pressure in the left corner. And Aussies are very fast upwind in breeze! We had been sailing slow boats for a while so that gave us an early, sharp lesson in prioritising pressure over shifts in skiffs and dialing down the tack rate!

Flexibility

Your race plan should never be totally fixed or totally flexible but there is a big range between the two. In tidal conditions and steadier wind, your race plan will be more fixed. In shifty winds, your plan will be more flexible. So typically, you will have a more fixed plan with tidal sailing, sea sailing and more wind. You will have a more flexible plan inland and in lighter winds

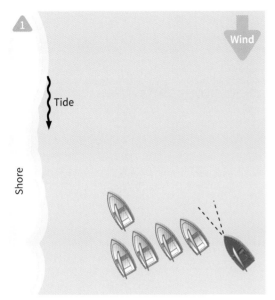

Move into high groove to establish a lane

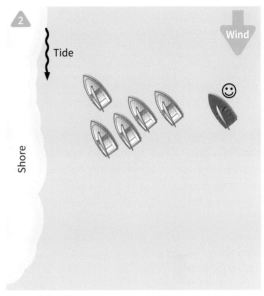

You will then be in a strong position

The most flexible plans should be in light winds on small lakes. Known as 'tack when it flaps', you should still have a plan for the race but it should be quickly overridden by windshifts. Tack when the front of the jib flaps as that indicates a big header. If your boat tacks well (e.g. an Enterprise), you might tack on the slightest shift when the front telltales are just lifting.

However, even on a small lake, there are typically wind bends and patterns which are 'gain features' which should form part of your plan. Gain features are wind patterns which are consistently in play on every leg such as a wind bend or convergence due to land.

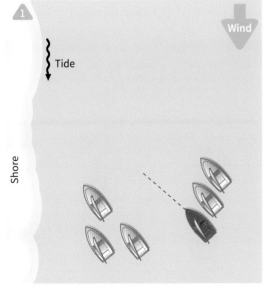

A lower mode is needed here to give you cleaner air

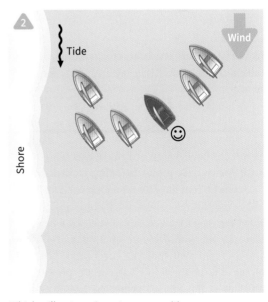

Which will put you in a stronger position

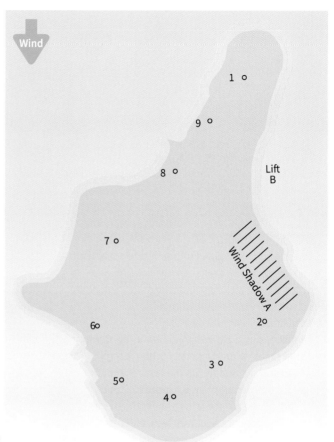

" At my learning ground and home club for many years, Frensham Pond Sailing Club, there are many gain features.

One of the most distinct is the beat from 3 to 9 where there is a mini headland two thirds of the way up the beat. Whilst shifts and pressure will rule, a game plan on this course would be to head a little left early on to avoid the worst of wind shadow A. Then head right to pick up the lift from shore B.

However, Frensham Pond is surrounded by trees so the wind is shifty and patchy. So your plan should be highly flexible. You should take the shifts or pressure which are right at the time whilst having your plan in the back of your mind.

When the wind is stable, your game plan should be relatively set with shifts and pressure feeding into it. "

Even on Frensham Pond you can have a race plan

Laylines

As you plan your first beat, conventional thinking tells you to avoid hitting laylines early for 2 key reasons:

- It limits your tactical options. You lose as a result of any windshift after you've hit the layline: a lift means you have overlaid; a header means boats below you make a gain.
- It leaves you prone to being tacked on and having to eat dirty air for a long period.

However, as with all tactics, this is not a hard and fast rule. As ever, pressure and shifts are king. If you are confident that you are on the best shift of the day or there is clearly more pressure on one side of the course, hitting the layline can pay handsomely. In very light winds, there is often

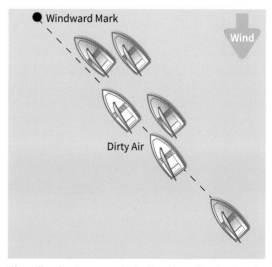

The yellow boats are on the layline, but sailing in dirty air

more wind at the edges of the course. Light wind is easily disturbed. Not only that, dirty wind also has a greater effect in light airs when it can be a struggle to keep airflow attached to your sails. Any disturbance to that (like dirty wind) upsets the fine balance. So hitting the laylines early can pay more in light winds, especially when it is steady and you are down the fleet. However, light winds are often shifty so then it is usually best to avoid hitting the laylines too early to manage the risk.

It is much harder to score a consistent series in light airs because the corners pay more and the wind is more fickle. But this is the same problem for everyone so, if you can deliver some semblance of consistency in light airs, you will do well overall.

How you deal with laylines should vary by boat and the length of the course. In boats that tack well, you should avoid hitting laylines too early as that limits your tactical options. In boats that don't tack well (generally fast boats), you should over lay slightly to avoid potentially unnecessary extra tacks.

The Overall First Beat Plan

Your first beat plan should not be set in stone as the wind and fleet positioning is constantly changing which is why every race is different and interesting! You should also think about some variations on your plan A (for example, if you are leebowed out the start will you pinch to find a lane, go low for a lane or tack). Once you have a plan, working through scenarios in your head (or combined heads if you have a crew) will allow you to react quickly to events, stay in control of your race and focus during the race on boatspeed rather than being absorbed in evaluating tactical options. A top crew can really help with this.

Here are some example first beat plans and moves in case of variations against the plan:

Left paying, heavily tidal

In this case, the first boat to the shore will lead. You should be the boat nearest the pin end but back off if you are seeking a safe start. If you execute

a poor start, you should be looking for a lane out left. A gap to leeward is really key out the start if it can be found as you will have to live with your lane for some time. If there is some distance until you reach the shore, this lane is even more important.

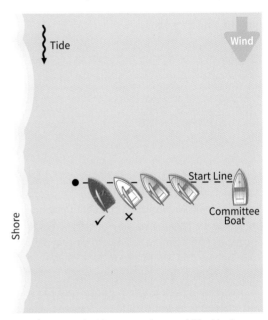

Be at the pin end with a gap to leeward (like blue) – yellow will struggle to find a lane

Alternative plans – if you lose your lane out the start (leebowed or someone sails over the top of you):

*   Depending on where other boats are, you may well choose to sail high and hang onto the lane to reach the shore still among the leaders.
*   If there is a lane to leeward, you may choose to sail low and re-establish a lane.
*   Or if there is space, you might quickly double tack to create a new lane.

A quick assessment of these options is needed with any just-passable lane out left good enough with left paying this heavily. Knowing your boat helps make this decision. Some boats foot well, some pinch well and some tack well. Others don't. Knowing this shapes your tactical options and your plan.

Left paying, very shifty and gusty

You should aim to take advantage of the paying side of the course by starting near the pin end. In these conditions, it is crucial that you have room to tack as early as possible. Your starting plan should be as described on p20 for a pin-biased line but with middle paying.

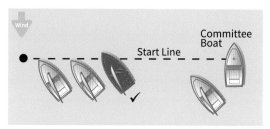

Be near the pin end, but with room to tack

As soon as you have started, you should be looking for space to tack. That is typically created by squeezing the boats to windward so they fall into your leebow and are forced to tack or slow down and lose height, creating space to tack.

You should seek to get in phase with the shifts and gusts as soon as possible. You need to get your head out of the boat early to start spotting shifts and pressure coming down the course. Once you are in phase, you should be very willing to take significant ducks on boats around you to remain in phase.

Opposition moves and countermoves:

* Be prepared to sacrifice short-term distance to stick to your route plan. You should have in your head how flexible or fixed your route plan is. That governs how much distance you are prepared to sacrifice to stick to the plan. For example, if right is very clearly paying upwind you may choose to duck a lot of starboard tackers to head right. On the other hand, if you are unsure which way will pay, you may choose to tack and leebow a starboard boat that you can't cross, as long as that works with the shift / pressure pattern, rather than take a significant duck and lose critical distance. A few ducks can add up to the difference between a top 5

windward mark rounding and being out the top 10, especially on a short beat.
* You have tactical advantage if you approach the windward mark on starboard. In the final 1/3 of the beat, you should start to adjust your route

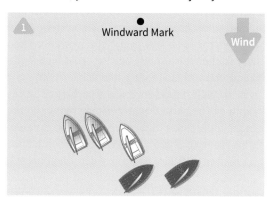

As you get closer to the windward mark there is a tactical advantage being on the right

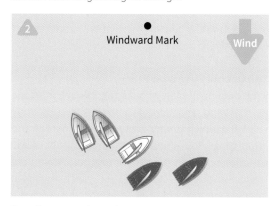

So yellow may also tack onto port

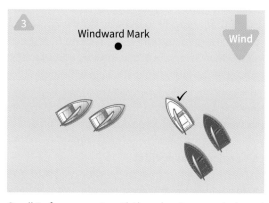

So all 3 of you come in with the advantage on starboard

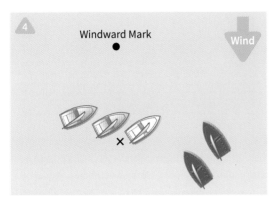

If yellow had not tacked onto port at that stage, he would be in a much weaker position when approaching the mark

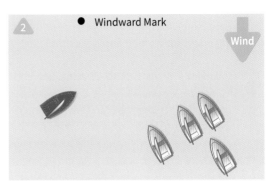

In which case, approaching in clear wind on port may be better

plan to end up on the right hand side of your opposition – unless, of course, pressure / shifts heavily favour the left. However, if you have space around you then you should approach the windward mark on the tack giving the best pressure and shifts.

• If you are sailing in a tight pack up the first beat, then a starboard approach pays most of the time. However, if everyone knows this, the starboard layline can become very congested. In this case, you either need to tack just above the line of boats approaching the windward mark on starboard to ensure you have a clear lane, or approach the layline late, but this is high risk.

• Finding a clear lane on the starboard layline can mean sailing a lot of extra distance. In this case, an approach on port can pay but is higher risk. If the starboard layline is congested, you should approach outside the 3-boat-length circle as you sacrifice many of your rights if you tack inside the 3-boat-length circle for a windward mark (rule 18.3).

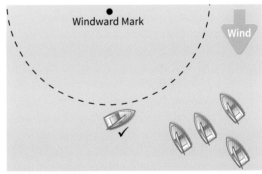

If you approach on port, do so outside the 3-boat-length circle

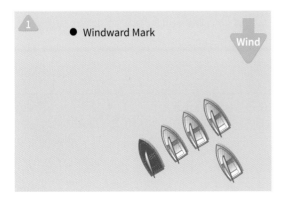

If everyone approaches on the starboard layline it can be very congested = slow

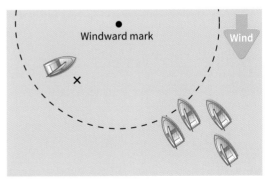

Inside the 3-boat-length circle you have few rights

Below are some examples of first beat plans, including ones that worked and ones that failed!

In race 7 of the 2014 RS400 Nationals at the fantastic venue of Mounts Bay, we were sailing in a 70 boat fleet with a short gate and first beat. We did not know which way would pay. Given this information, we chose to start on the right hand side of the pack because, with the short gate and first beat, an early start would be a big gamble as it typically takes some time to find a lane to tack out of a gate start.

So our plan A was to start late in space. With the short first beat, our expectation was that the fleet would end up stacked up towards the port layline because of the difficulty of finding space to tack early out of a gate. We would start late to avoid being boxed in on the left hand side of the beat, and look for an early tack out to achieve the mantra of bow out on the long tack. We would be happy to take a duck to tack onto port before most of the fleet.

As it transpired, we executed a good start late out of the gate as planned. However, a top team (Mike Simms / Rich Brown), starting a few boats up from us, also pulled off a good start so we could not tack. We sailed low for around 10 lengths to generate space for a good tack and tacked. We then ducked very close to the transom of our rival to ensure that they couldn't tack on our wind without us quickly leebowing them.

This got us bow out on the long tack and first to the layline which is where we could use our starboard advantage to narrowly lead around the windward mark – front cover of Helming to Win!

Lark Class gate start

We (blue) could not tack because of yellow

We sailed low to generate room to tack and ducked yellow's transom very close

Ducking very close meant that, if yellow tacked, they would be quickly leebowed

So yellow tacked later, giving us space and the right hand advantage

❝ *In race 4 of a Merlin Rocket open meeting at Hayling Island in 2015, we thought left would pay as there had been slightly more pressure on that side of the course and there had been a lift into the windward mark on port some of the time. We got a nice start and were able to tack and cross the fleet to consolidate our lead – the classic textbook move. Our first mistake! It was a very short first beat on which some of the fleet weren't far off planing upwind so every tack was costly. After our tack out of the start, we were heading right and sailed into a 10 degree header. It was big enough to take but it swung back as we came into the windward mark. With 2 extra tacks and coming back into the boats from the left on a header, we ended up 13th at the windward mark.* ❞

We (blue) got a nice start and were clear of the fleet, able to dictate

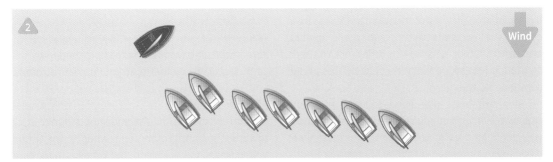

We followed conventional wisdom and tacked across the fleet to consolidate our lead, ignoring the fact that we thought left would pay

And so it proved: left paid and the extra tacks were costly

Even more so when we were headed on starboard

There were a few key lessons from this. We didn't stick to our plan A which cost us dearly. The shortness of the first beat in near planing conditions should have dictated a lower tack rate. And the last shift into the windward mark is the key one. It is critical because you cannot recover the places back on the next breeze oscillation as you often can if you are hit by an adverse windshift part way up the beat.

The last shift sets your position for the first downwind leg, often determining whether you will sail in nice clear wind and water or have to try to fight your way through the pack. If you are unsure which way the last shift will go, you should hedge your bets towards the middle of the pack while seeking the best pressure possible.

There is more scope to control the fleet and the race in slow boats. The effective tack rate is higher in slow boats providing more opportunities to be in control. Also, in boats which do not plane upwind, pressure differences make less difference to speed so there is less scope for gains once behind and in someone's cover.

In a fast boat, you need to keep attacking pressure even when you're ahead. In a slow boat you can defend harder because the losses are less if you fall out of phase with the shifts and pressure.

If you do run into a situation which is a total surprise and not part of your race plan, you sometimes need a fast response. In these scenarios, trust your instincts. They are formed from your past experiences so are usually right. If they prove wrong, review the situation and learn from it so your instincts are improved in the future.

Going into the last race of the 2011 OK Worlds, I was lying 4th overall and 3 points off the lead. My outcome objective was to win so I was willing to gamble to have a chance of the overall win knowing that meant the risk of dropping out of a tightly packed top 10. I had good pace in a force 2+ but had speed issues that week in under 6 knots. After a few hours postponement, the race started in just a few knots of wind.

Knowing that I was behind my outcome objective, and in my unfavoured conditions, I made the decision to *gamble hard right from the start. So I went for the high risk move of being the pin-end boat on a port-biased line in a big fleet. The start went well so I was able to tack onto port and get on top of most of the fleet early. But other sailors had also tacked onto port early and started wasting me with their superior speed. So I tacked out further to the left of the fleet having seen a little more wind out left.*

Normally, I would be exceptionally uncomfortable splitting from the fleet when in a top 5 position, especially on the first beat. However, this was the right call given my outcome objective. I got lucky and the wind out left kept building as I sailed further and further left. I rounded the windward mark with a good lead after a 4 tack beat: very rare in light and shifty winds in an OK. With my poor speed, my initial lead got ground back to a 4th by the finish but just enough to win overall! Happy days!

First Reach Plan

Your initial plan for the first reach is shaped by the same factors that determine your upwind strategy.

Attitude to Risk

If your race plan is low risk you should aim to stick towards the middle of the fleet, whilst trying to find a lane to sail in clear wind and waves. However, it is often impossible to find clear wind and waves around the middle of the fleet, especially if you are sailing in the pack. If so, it usually pays to head high to ensure clear wind and waves.

If your plan is high risk, your plan will tend towards a high or low route depending on the factors below. Going low is much higher risk than going high. Going low can result in losing many places if the wind heads or pressure fills in to windward resulting in you falling to leeward of the pack and being blanketed. The pack tends to go high so, if you also go high, your risk is reduced.

However, going low can pay handsomely and result in dramatic place changes. Going low is most likely to pay:
- On a broad leg
- In steadier wind
- With tide pushing to windward

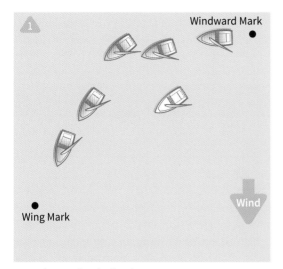

Going low is often high risk

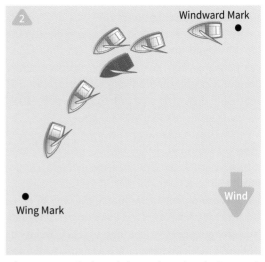

Whereas going high, with the pack tends to be lower risk

- If there is a chance that the wind will lift to make the leg even broader
- If the fleet is sailing a 'bendy banana' (i.e. lots of boats and the pack pushing high)

Leg Bias

If the first reach is tight, a high route generally pays because it is very hard to overtake to leeward on a tight reach due the position of the wind shadow.

Also, a header could cause the reach to become a fetch or even a beat, in which case you definitely don't want to be caught low.

If the reach is broad, the latter stages of the leg often become a near run because boats typically push high early in the reach seeking to overtake. So you should be looking for opportunities to find a low lane and consider going low from the start of the reach.

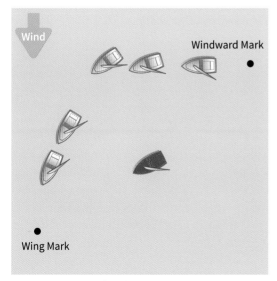

Going low can pay if the fleet goes very high

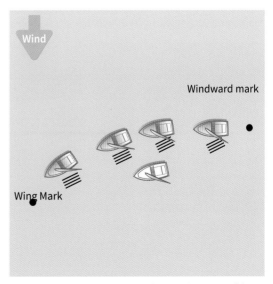

Going low on a tight reach rarely pays, because of the wind shadow

Next Mark Rounding Direction

On the first reach, the next mark is a gybe so going low gives you the inside overlap. On the second reach, going high gives you the inside overlap. So low is slightly more likely to pay on the first reach and high on the second to gain a potentially valuable inside overlap at the mark.

Tide

If there is significant tide, this should have a major impact on your route decision. If the tide is pushing you downwind, high is probably the way to go as the tide will cause the reach to be tighter. If the tide is pushing upwind, a low lane can pay dividends even on a reach that appears to be relatively tight as the tide can make that reach broad. On a long reach with tide, a transit can be very helpful for identifying the rhumb line (the straight line and shortest course between the marks).

Wind Pattern

You should be steering with the breeze downwind so working low in the gusts to increase the time you spend in gusts. This also means that you sail the broader, slower angles in more wind. You should be working high in the lulls to move on to the next gust as soon as possible. A wind bend or persistently more wind on one part of the race course can make

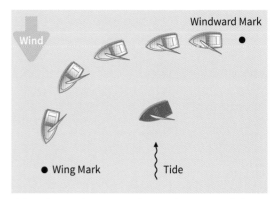

If the tide is pushing upwind, going low is a good idea

a high or low route favourable. In more unstable wind, a high route is safer because you won't be rolled by the pack to windward if new wind arrives above the fleet or the unstable wind heads in direction.

Waves

Waves are very quickly disrupted by the wakes of other boats. They are then much harder to surf. This means that clear water can be more important than clear wind when sailing downwind in significant waves, especially in marginal planing conditions. In general, clear waves are found higher on the reach, before they have been disturbed by other boats.

Waves flattened out on the back of a boat

Your Downwind Speed

If you are fast, you should seek to establish a lane above the pack and use your pace. Speed differences are greatest in marginal planing so it can pay to work high early (e.g. by delaying a spinnaker hoist, if you have one) to make a lane.

If you are slow, you will need to stay high to defend and prevent major place losses.

If your speed is average, try to work with the pack to sail the rhumb line and minimise the distance sailed.

The Overall First Reach Plan

So, in summary, there are many factors pointing towards going high on reaches. That is a good default position as high pays much more often than not. However, most of the fleet know this and, with many boats seeking a high lane, a banana of extra distance is quickly formed:

With this pattern likely to emerge, you should always have an eye on finding a lane on the rhumb line or at least a little lower than the pack.

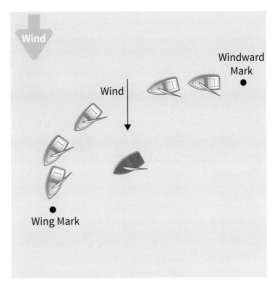

Blue has found a lane on the rhumb line

This is challenging as a wider lane is needed on reaches than upwind as both clear waves and wind are needed to sail fast. The wake off boats form a triangle of disturbed water which can be quite wide.

However, because finding a good lane away from the high route (often extra distance as the fleet sails a banana) is challenging, the gains from finding such a lane can be considerable.

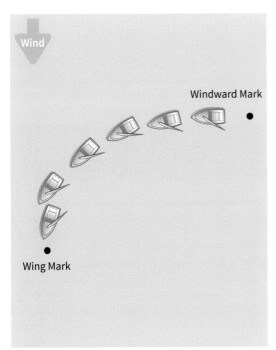

The classic 'bendy banana' on the reach with the fleet going very high

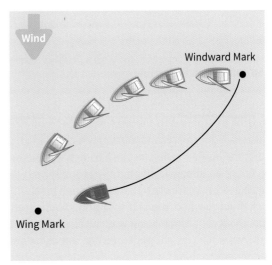

If you can get a lane, away from the pack, going low on the reach can pay dividends

The difficulty of finding reaching lanes is a major reason why the start and first beat are especially important in non-asymmetric boats. Windward mark positions are hard to change on the reaches in these types of boats and the fleet becomes much more spread out on the reaches.

In a spinnaker boat, the first reach can be tight so it is debatable whether to hoist the spinnaker or not. The safe option is to hoist late. If there are boats ahead, look at how they are managing with or without the spinnaker. If you are expecting a lift, hoist early. If you are expecting a header, hoist late or not at all. As you approach the windward mark, remind yourself whether you are lifted or headed on starboard to help with this decision.

Struggling with spinnaker on a tight reach

Second Reach Plan

The same principles for deciding your route plan that were applied to the first reach decision are also valid for the second reach. The one change is that the inside overlap for the next mark rounding is obtained from going high. So it generally pays to go high even more often than on the first reach!

If you do find yourself low, you should start planning your moves a fair way out to ensure that you work high for an inside overlap. But if you are confident that you will round in clear water, not having boats inside you, there is no need to waste distance working high.

Run Plan: Non-spinnaker Boats

In non-spinnaker boats, in all but light winds, you should be steering quite big angles on the run and seeking to use the waves. Clear water is key to enable wide steering angles. This generally means having some separation from the pack or a fairly wide lane because other boats distort and flatten out waves. Finding a rhythm down waves can be tricky enough without the hindrance of disturbed water. So avoiding the wakes of other boats is preferable on runs.

Your first principle should be to steer to the best pressure and waves where possible. Just as when forming an upwind plan, you should use these factors to determine your plan A for the run:

Attitude To Risk

If your race plan is low risk you should aim to stick towards the middle of the fleet, whilst trying to find a lane to sail in clear wind and waves. However, it can be impossible to find clear wind and waves around the middle of the fleet. In this scenario, it pays to head away from the pack to find clear wind and waves whilst minimising separation from the pack or ideally finding a lane within the pack.

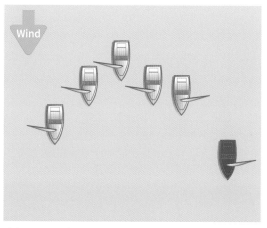

If there is no clear wind in the pack, separate from it slightly

If your plan is high risk, you should aim for one side of the course determined by the factors below.

Leg Bias

As for upwind, this is a main driver of your route decision. Typically, you will spend more time on one gybe than the other. As for upwind, you should aim to sail the long gybe first and, for as long as possible, in clear wind. So, if the run is starboard-gybe biased, you will be looking to get to the right of the fleet to minimise the risk of being blanketed if the wind shifts.

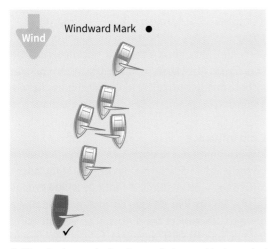

Sailing the long gybe first is usually best, with clear wind

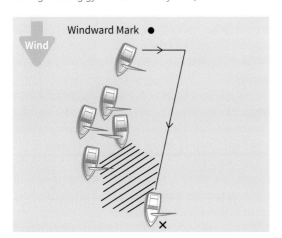

If you sail the short gybe first you will generally end up in dirty wind

By sailing the long gybe first, the law of averages is on your side and you have more time to choose the best angle to sail the short gybe. It is also likely

that sailing the long gybe first will give you clearer wind.

As ever, this isn't a hard and fast rule as shifts and pressure are still key. So, if there is more pressure by taking the short gybe first, that can pay. Or an expected windshift can drive a decision to take the short gybe first.

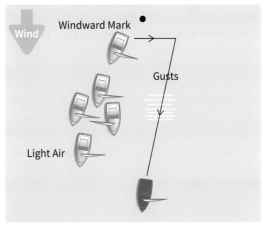

But more pressure may mean it is worth sailing the short gybe first

If there is significant tide, this will impact which gybe is the long one and needs to be taken into account. A leg that may appear to be a run can, in reality, be turned into a reach by strong tide. In this case, the 'run' plan should be made using the factors that determine a reach plan (outlined above).

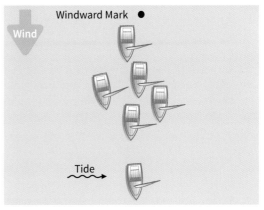

Tide across the course can make a run into a reach

Wind Pattern

You should have an idea of the wind pattern and your run game plan before you start the run. You'll have your wind tracking from before the start and, more importantly, what you have learnt in the race so far. As for upwind, understanding the weather forecast to have an idea where the next shift may come from can help. However, weather forecasts tend to be over quite a long period and a run is typically no more than 10 minutes long so short-term factors are usually more relevant. You should understand the impact of land and clouds on the breeze and whether it is an unstable or stable wind and how a sea breeze may develop and impact on the gradient wind.

In light winds, there is often more breeze at the edge of the course where it isn't so disturbed by the fleet. So, sailing to one side of the fleet is sometimes required.

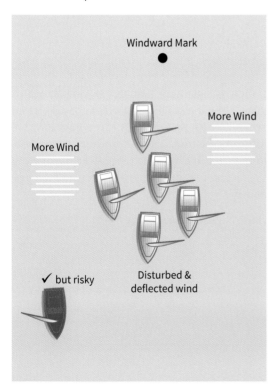

In light winds there is often more wind at the edges, so sailing to one side of the fleet may be sensible, although it can be a bit of a risk

You should constantly be checking for pressure across the course. So you need to perfect your boat handling and straight line speed, enabling you to spend a fair bit of time looking backwards whilst sailing fast. And staying upright! Pressure matters most in marginal planing conditions as the speed difference between sub-planing and planing is typically big.

Tide

A simple and fairly reliable rule is the opposite way will typically pay on the run to the beat. Be mindful of the time though as, of course, tidal flows change over time. Also keep in mind that tide changes inshore first so the paying route will change inshore before it changes out to sea / in deeper waters.

Land Influence

It is rare that land doesn't have a major influence on the wind on dinghy racing courses. Many books have been written about it (notably *Wind Strategy* in the *Sail to Win* series), so justice couldn't be done to the subject here! As well as the impact of land on wind bends and convergence, you should consider how stable the wind is. For example, offshore winds tend to be more unstable which moves your strategy towards gybing on shifts down the middle of the course.

Waves

Waves are very quickly disrupted by the wakes of other boats. They are then much harder to surf. This means that clear water is more important than clear wind when sailing downwind in significant waves, especially in marginal planing conditions. In general, clear waves are found to one side of the course away from the pack but often less risky lanes can be found in the pack.

There are sometimes significantly more waves or choppier water on one part of the course which is a good part of the course to be on downwind, unless they are standing waves which are hard to surf over. Choppy water may also indicate shallow water or a tide line which may be useful information for your tidal strategy.

The Overall Run Plan (non-spinnaker)

Based on these six factors, you should form an idea of which way you think will pay on the run. It is critical to be honest with yourself. Being not sure is absolutely fine and pretty common. That in itself is a good thing as you can then attempt to manage risk effectively and stick to the middle of the fleet. However, managing that risk is harder on a run as sticking to the middle can just lead to dirty wind and water resulting in place losses.

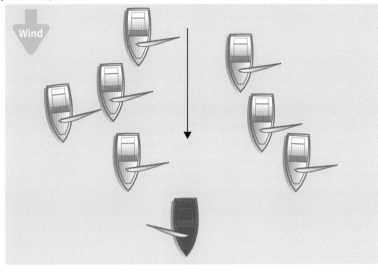

The ideal position: with the fleet, but with a lane

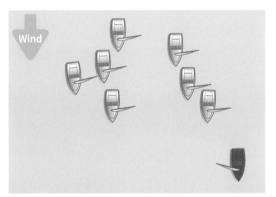

Being on the edge of the fleet gives you a clear lane, but can be risky

Particularly if the wind shifts adversely

In a single-hander you can sail by the lee to find a new lane, slightly away from the pack.

If you are blanketed in a single-hander

You can sail by the lee to move out of the disturbed air

And into a new, clear lane

If it is an exceptionally windy day, you may choose to reduce risk by dropping your gybe rate and restricting to one gybe or even no gybes by chicken gybing (tacking round). With a leeward gate, judging the layline for the left hand buoy (facing downwind) can be tricky but this is the buoy you are aiming to round to save on a gybe. (In a spinnaker boat, you should bias towards overlaying as you can always drop the spinnaker early and tight reach into the left-hand leeward buoy.) In a single-hander, broad reaching is a much safer angle than running so, again, bias towards overlaying the leeward mark. If you underlay, you will have to gybe again to the right-hand buoy which increases risk.

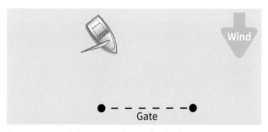

Best approach is to come in on the layline

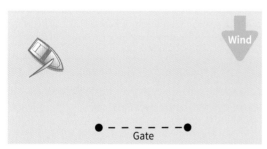

Alternatively overlay because you can tight reach into the buoy

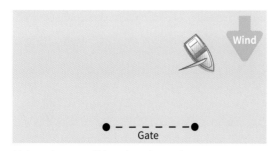

Not great – you will have to gybe again

Clear wind and water are crucial downwind in symmetric boats. So you should know the gybing angles of your boat. This will help you understand where the clear lanes will be on the next gybe and so enable you to time your gybe for a clear lane whilst, of course, using pressure and shifts.

Perfect, in clear wind

If you gybe early…

You will still be in clear wind

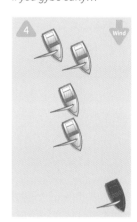

But if you gybe late…

You will be in dirty air

Awareness of these gybing angles and how the fleet is distributed allows you to map out where the clear wind lanes might be a few moves in advance.

These clear lanes are dynamic as boats gybe off at different times. So keeping your head out of the boat and adjusting your plan is essential. Your aim is to do this whilst also sailing fast and tracking pressure and shifts. As ever, this requires a lot of practice. A great crew really helps!

Run Plan: Asymmetric Boats

The same factors as above apply to deciding your route plan. However, in asymmetrics pressure is much more important as sailing in more wind means going faster and lower, the dream ticket!

There are 6 rules for asymmetric runs which I always remind myself of before jumping back into an asymmetric after time out in other boats:

1. Bow out on the long gybe generally pays. This is similar to the golden rule upwind that bow out on the long tack pays. This positioning means that you gain on most shifts unless your tactical analysis clearly points to being on a different part of the course.

2. Splitting from the fleet downwind in an asymmetric is a big gamble because separation quickly opens up so potential gains and losses are big. Greater separation means increased scope for gains and losses. Also, asymmetrics sail significantly faster and lower in more pressure: a double gain. So, if you split and there is more pressure on the other side of the course, you lose big time!

However, clear air and water in an asymmetric is key. Asymmetrics kick out a lot of dirty wind from their large spinnakers

So, clear air and water typically outweigh the other rules. But ideally, you will have clear air and water, not split from the pack and be bow out on the long gybe. If you have these ideas in your head, they will usually happen, whereas no plan usually means a lot of time in dirty wind and water.

In an asymmetric, splitting too far from the fleet is risky

If the wind heads, you are out on a limb

But if it lifts you will be looking good

Better to stay closer to the pack, still in clear air, but de-risked

If the wind heads, you are still OK

And if it lifts, it is also OK

3. Avoid getting boxed in (i.e. sailing towards laylines too early or sailing underneath a pack of boats), especially in a big fleet when you are sailing in the pack. As you plan your downwind route, you need to avoid being boxed in.

   If you do end up boxed in, you just have to eat dirt as effectively as possible and vow never to put yourself in this situation again!! The best option is to work high and try to regain a lane, even though this means sailing extra distance and possibly a double gybe to lay the leeward mark again. If you are going to be boxed in for only a short time, it can be worth living with it to avoid sailing extra distance. You will be sailing in unstable wind so you will need to make more sail adjustments, trim more and move more as the wind fluctuates. You need to do all this smoothly to keep the boat gliding and not upset its balance, especially in light airs. The wind is slowed so you will need to sail slightly higher angles and with less kicker for a more forgiving leech.

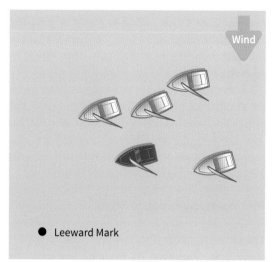

Avoid being boxed in

4. Aim to approach the leeward mark on the starboard layline when in the pack to gain mark room. Approach on the port layline when ahead to give time for a good kite drop. There is big scope for gains if you approach the leeward mark on starboard inside the 3-boat-length circle as you probably have mark room on the whole fleet.

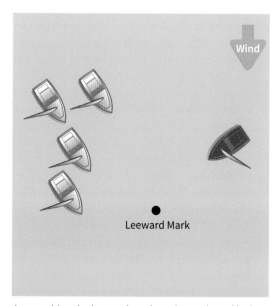

Approaching the leeward mark on the starboard layline gives you mark room

5. Aim to gybe at the end of a gust so you sail across it again and re-use it. If you need to gybe for tactical reasons or to avoid other boats etc., you should aim to do that just before the gust starts losing pressure so you gybe back across the gust and re-use it.

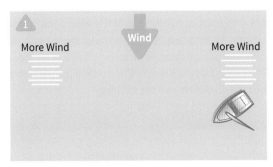

You want to stay in the gust

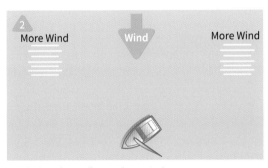

So don't sail out of it into less wind

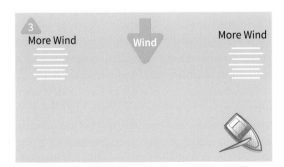

Gybe before you are out of the gust, so you stay in it

Pressure bands are dynamic so you need to keep your head out of the boat. Being able to watch developments helps you understand how quickly gusts are moving down the course – some are more static and some move faster.

6. Avoid gybing in lulls where possible because this tends to prolong the 'lull pain'! Gybing when you've just sailed through a lull can spell trouble as that often means that you will sail back through the lull again.

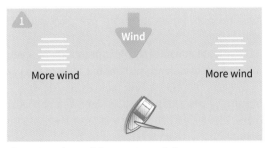

If you do sail out of the gust into a lull…

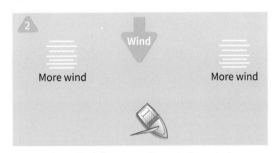

Don't gybe in the lull or you will stay in less wind

If another boat is potentially forcing you to gybe back across a lull, a substantial course alteration can be worthwhile to avoid this horrible gybe and also leave your opponent sailing in the lull.

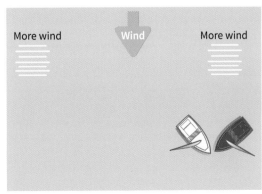

Avoid being forced to gybe into a lull – yellow is better going behind blue into the gust than gybing into the lull

As ever, pressure and shifts can trump all these rules!

The range of angles in a spinnaker boat, even an asymmetric one, are narrower than in a single-hander so clear decision making is more important as it is harder to steer your way out of a wrong decision and separation from the pack quickly opens up.

If you are ahead of the fleet or a pack, or if you are looking to defend, you should soak low early in the leg. This will deliver 'golden positioning' – putting yourself between the fleet and the next mark. Ideally, you should execute this whilst still maintaining a clear wind lane.

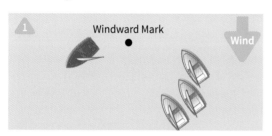

If you round the windward mark ahead

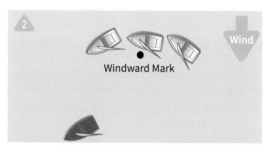

Soak low, or double gybe, to put yourself between the fleet and the next mark

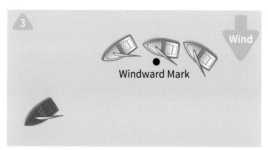

If you just charge on, you are separating from the fleet and putting yourself in a risky position

Run Plan: Symmetric Spinnaker Boats

The principles are very similar to those for asymmetrics but the gybing angles are smaller. So this typically means fewer gybes which makes each gybe decision more critical. The route plan is more important with fewer gybes because you are more locked into your early decisions. With smaller gybing angles, you should be looking in different places for pressure.

This is a key transition when switching between boats – where to look downwind.

 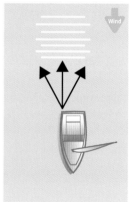

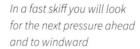

In a fast skiff you will look for the next pressure ahead and to windward

But in a slower boat you will be looking more behind you

Conclusion

You should have a race plan at all times during the race which should constantly be re-evaluated.

However, while it is great to have a race plan, ultimately fast sailing and good windshift and gust selection will win the day! So don't get too hung up on positioning. If you see good pressure or a nice shift: go for it, but keep the race plan in the back of your mind. With a lot of practice in high quality big fleets, you have to think less about tactics as they become routine and instinctive. This enables you to focus back on finding the rhythm of shifts and pressure. When you are in the rhythm, you can then focus on boatspeed again – going fast the right way is always good!

CHAPTER 5

Mark Tactics

This chapter describes the ideal boat positioning and tactics for mark roundings. However, these guidelines should not be used dogmatically. Once again, boatspeed and windshifts remain king so it can pay to deviate significantly from these tactics. You can sail around a well-positioned opponent who is sailing slowly or missing shifts or pressure. So don't forget to keep your head out of the boat and look for a gust, windshift or overtaking lane when deploying these tactics. Your aim is for these tactics to become instinctive through lots of race training. Then you can focus on sailing fast whilst deploying smart tactics, a highly effective combination!

Overall Principles of Mark Tactics

Communication is key to ensuring that you avoid difficult protests or potentially falling out with your fellow competitors. By sharing with people your intentions on whether you are overlapped etc., you can quickly tell if the other sailor agrees or you have a disagreement on your hands. You can then make an informed decision on the appropriate course in the circumstances, depending on who the onus of proof is on and how much risk you are willing to take at that stage of the regatta.

Faultless boathandling is a key foundation for all of these moves and is covered in *Helming to Win*. In this chapter, some punchier defensive and overtaking moves are described. These more punchy tactics should be used judiciously. Some of them are potentially major distance losers and so should only be used when beating one opponent is critical or there is a big gap to the next boat at a late stage in a race.

You should have as many **tools in your tactics box** as possible so it is good be aware of these moves. But every tool should be used appropriately. You wouldn't use hammer to undo a bolt (well I might, my short book on *Boat Maintenance to Lose* is not in progress!). If you have the opportunity, team or match racing is the best, rapid schooling for boat-on-boat tactics and learning some of the more punchy moves. And team and match racing are a lot of fun!

As you read the overtaking sections, keep in mind that these are the moves you may need to defend against.

Thorough **rules knowledge** is also important to use these tactical tools without taking inappropriate risks. You should be aware of when you have the upper hand (i.e. the onus of proof is on your opponent) and when you are exposed (i.e. when you carry the burden of proof if there is a protest).

Key situations are:

- If there is a collision between a starboard tack and port tack boat, the port tack boat is usually guilty until proven innocent. The port tacker will need to prove the starboard tacker did not allow them an opportunity to avoid a collision, such as tacking in their water.
- If there is a collision between a windward and leeward boat, the windward boat is typically guilty until proven innocent. The windward boat will need to prove that the leeward boat luffed violently without giving them opportunity to keep clear.
- If there is a collision on a mark rounding, the boat which established or broke the overlap (i.e. is claiming a change in overlap) is guilty until proven innocent.

Being aware of the risk of each move and how much risk is appropriate at that point in your race or series will avoid needless protests or disqualifications.

> *At the 2015 Merlin Rocket Nationals in race 5, we were lying 2nd approaching the first gybe mark. The leading boat gybed wide so we took an opportunity to gain a windward passing lane on the second reach. The leeward boat then luffed hard and, in my view, we didn't have time to avoid a collision. However, we were windward boat and had already blown our discard. So we took the appropriate conservative action of taking a 720° penalty.*

Port-hand Windward Mark

Attack

You can attack a boat in front by watching where they tack for the starboard layline. If they are below, on or only just above the layline, tack around half a boat length above their line. Then, if your opponent cannot lay the mark, you can attack by stopping them tacking and forcing them to gybe out. This can work even if they are initially above the layline if a header comes through.

Having a strong handle on the shift pattern and what shift is coming next will help with your positioning. If you expect the wind to lift, your opponent will probably lay the mark. In this case, avoid wasted distance by tacking right on their transom. You can tack to leeward if the lift is expected to be big and you are near the mark and so can live with some dirty wind and still lay the mark.

Tacking half a boat length above their line is a good attack position

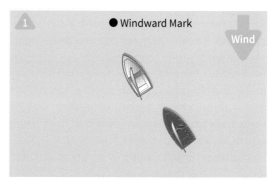

If you are expecting a lift, do not go so far before tacking on the layline

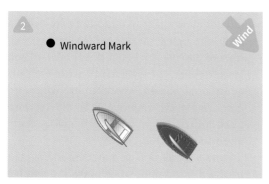

If a header comes in, they will not be able to lay the mark and they may have to gybe out

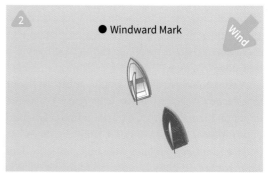

When the lift comes you will have saved wasted distance by tacking earlier

How far above their line you need to tack depends on how long you will need to hold your lane for and how hard it is to hold a lane in the class that you are sailing in the current conditions. It is easier to hold a lane in steady wind and water, harder in chop and shifty wind. For example, if you are tacking behind your opponent a couple of lengths out from the mark in a boat that holds its lane well, you can probably tack right on their transom to save sailing extra distance.

If you are tacking a long way out from the mark, then you will need to hold a lane for a long time despite potential headers, bad waves etc., so a boat length or so gap may make more sense.

This is another time where the ability to hold narrow lanes is a distance gainer. Being able to hold narrow lanes is a critical skill for being able to make recoveries from sub-standard starts, especially in a big fleet.

If another boat has tacked above the starboard layline, you could choose to tack underneath them and, if you make it round the mark, you can make a nice place gain.

This is a risky move as a poor tack, loss of speed or windshift can all land you in trouble especially in a crowded pack if you can't lay the mark after all.

So you should be well aware of the appropriate risk to be taking at that point in the race / series when deciding whether to tack under another boat on the starboard layline.

Defence

To defend against potentially being blocked out below the layline, you should tack just above the starboard layline to give yourself some room for manoeuvre in case you misjudge the layline or a header comes through. Of course that involves a small loss of distance so you should consider that in context of your attitude to risk in that race, the windshift pattern and your ability to hold a lane (e.g. that is harder in choppy waves).

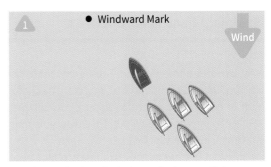

Blue has tacked on the layline, which is an efficient use of distance, but could be risky

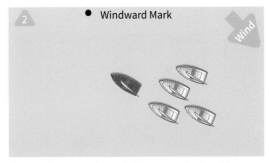

If a header comes through, blue is in a bad position

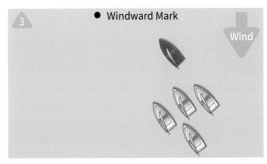

If blue tacks above the layline, he has lost distance, but it is low risk

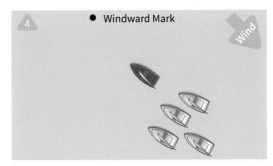

If a header comes through, blue is still safe

Starboard-hand Windward Mark

Attack

Although not often used, this is a great mark for opening up attacking options. You can attack the boat or boats in front by positioning yourself just above the starboard layline. This way you may gain an inside overlap. Or you may make life tricky for the boat in front as they will need to tack onto port to round the mark whilst you charge in on starboard! This attack isn't a certain place gainer but it at least puts pressure on your opposition.

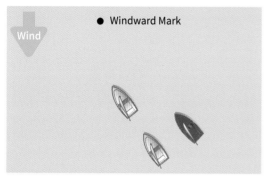

Blue is in a strong position approaching a starboard-hand mark

Defence

To defend you should approach the windward mark on or just above the layline to prevent any boats sneaking inside you. As you luff to tack, ensure that the boat behind doesn't squeeze inside you. If an opponent does sneak inside you, avoid a collision but immediately hail protest for taking mark room they did not have and then ask them to do a 720° turn.

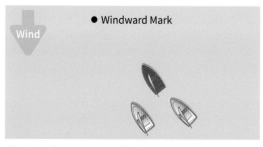

Blue is well positioned defensively

Counter-attack

If the boat ahead has defended well, keep the pressure on by sticking very close to them. A poorly executed luff or tack could result in them infringing rule 13 (tacking boat has no rights).

Gybe Mark

As with any mark rounding, forward planning is critical to gain or hold places. You should be planning your route to gain as many inside overlaps as possible. If you are high of other boats, ensure that you are confident that you will break clear of any inside boats. Or make an early decision that overlaps aren't going to be broken so start working low in advance of the gybe mark to gain inside overlaps.

If you find you are at risk of being caught outside a group of boats, it is usually worth slowing down and seeking an inside overlap. Being caught outside a pack often sets up a bad start to the next leg by limiting your tactical options, on top of the places lost at the time.

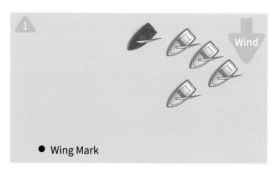

Blue is not going to get an inside overlap

And will be on the outside at the mark if he does nothing

Blue should make an early decision to work low

And aim to get an inside overlap on some of the boats

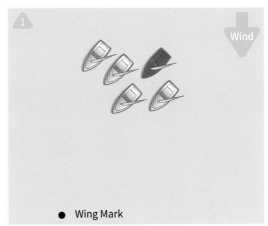

If you are in a weak position like blue

Gybing out can be a solution

On a very broad first reach, where boats are caught high, a double gybe can be a very effective move to gain an inside overlap. Visualising the position you need to be in at the 3-boat-length circle will help you plan the moves to arrive in that place.

Your exit from the gybe mark is important as this sets up your initial lane for the next leg. If the next reach is a tight one, exiting the gybe mark high is especially important.

If there has been a significant windshift, the second reach can become very broad or even a run. If that is the case, your tactical options open up considerably and need to be decided well before the gybe mark.

> " At the 2014 Merlin Rocket Nationals, we had a very tight battle with Stuart Bithell & Tom Pygall. It went down to the last race which started well for us as we led to the first gybe mark with Stu & Tom in 3rd. We gybed at the gybe mark as did Tim Fells & Chris Downham in 2nd. In gusty and patchy winds bouncing

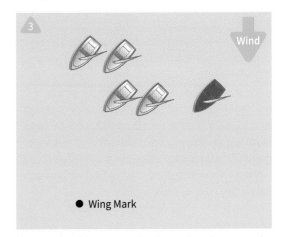

You may be able to get an inside overlap when you gybe back

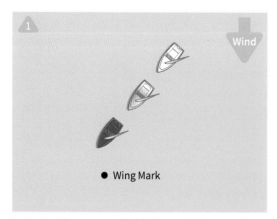

In the deciding race, we (in blue) were looking good, with Stuart Bithell (yellow) in third

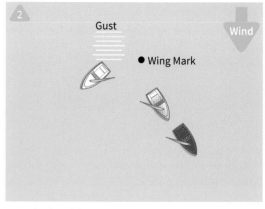

We gybed as did second placed Tim Fells, but Stuart stayed in a gust and did not gybe

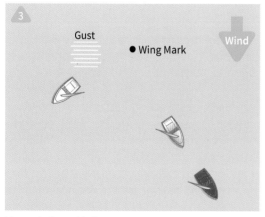

He carried on with the gust

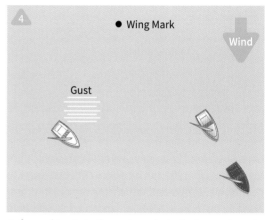

Before gybing in to the next mark at a faster angle and more pressure to win the race and the championships

off the hills of Looe, Stu & Tom picked up a gust just before the gybe mark and started planing whilst we wallowed in a lull. Super-quick thinking and a focus on gusts and pressure above conventional tactical rules led them to carry on in that gust for several boat lengths after the gybe mark before gybing. Even with the benefit of hindsight, there was no defence against this brilliant move. They then gybed and moved into 1st as they sailed a tighter, faster angle into the leeward mark in more pressure never to be caught.

This was a great example of Stu trusting his gut instincts. It is an example of shifts and pressure trumping anything written in tactics books!

Hard Defence

If a boat is just overlapped on you as you approach the gybe mark, an aggressive defence is to work as low as possible to give yourself space to luff just before entering the 3-boat-length circle to break the overlap through changing the angle of your transom.

The timing of this luff makes or breaks the move. It needs to be executed just before you enter the 3-boat-length circle to break the overlap. If you luff too early, you will slow down and have to bear off again to make the mark, so actually increasing the overlap. If you execute the move too late, the overlap is already established at the 3-boat-length circle.

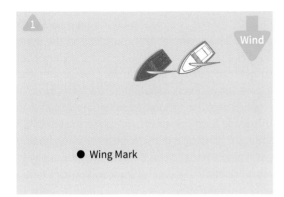

If approaching the gybe mark with a boat overlapped inside you

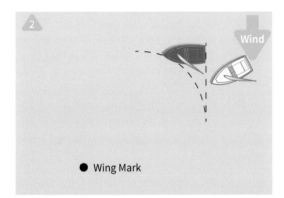

A hard luff when approaching the zone can break the overlap

This is a high risk manoeuvre because the onus of proof in a protest is on the boat which breaks the overlap. If the boat you have broken the overlap on still hails "mark room", so has effectively not acknowledged your cunning manoeuvre, you are best to give room unless high risk is appropriate at the time (e.g. it is the last race of an event and you need to beat this boat to achieve your results objective). The challenge with this move is that it is hard to judge 3-boat-lengths of distance so everyone has a different opinion on where it is. A good witness or nearby jury is usually needed to win this protest.

A safe but aggressive tactic is to perform this move, give room if claimed by your opponent and then protest.

Aim to work low early on a boat potentially

seeking to gain an inside overlap, the leeward boat will end up in your shadow as you will come into the mark on a tighter angle. That will make overtaking or gaining an overlap for the leeward boat more challenging.

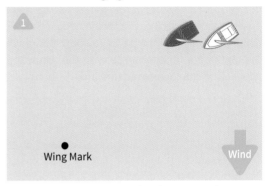

If approaching the gybe mark with someone threatening to be overlapped

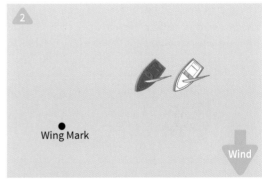

Seek to go low

So you can then luff, give them dirty wind and potentially break the overlap

However, a smart competitor will sail their proper course on the rhumb line. As windward boat, you are obliged to keep clear (rule 11). A canny competitor may find a fair reason to sail above the rhumb line justifying this as their proper course due to more pressure, better waves etc. up high. That will then make it easier for them to gain water in the final stages of the leg as you both approach the mark on a broader angle with the windward boat's wind shadow moved forward.

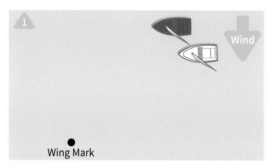

A smart competitor with an overlap will seek to go high (blue is windward boat)

With more chance of an overlap when you bear away and less chance of wind shadow

Port-hand Leeward Mark

Your exit plan dictates how you should round and enter the leeward mark. So you should have your exit plan in mind some way before the leeward mark. Your exit plan is where you want to be heading after the leeward mark – left, right or flexible.

If you are looking for an early tack out from the leeward mark (left / middle paying or your plan is flexible) then it is critical that you gain an inside overlap and secure a tight rounding on the mark even if that means sacrificing some distance, or sometimes even a place, before you enter the 3-boat-length circle to gain that inside berth.

It is unusual to look for anything other than the inside berth. However, in a major melee and if the right hand side of the course is paying heavily (with a port-hand leeward mark) then it can pay to round outside a group, so long as you can find a lane and keep speed on.

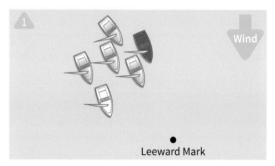

Usually you would want to get the inside overlap, as blue has

And round tight to the mark

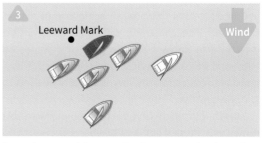

But going round the outside of a major melee (as yellow has) may be good if the right is paying

Also, if the wind is very shifty (e.g. sailing on a small lake), it is highly likely that everyone will tack pretty quickly so lanes will open up. So then it may be worth rounding as an outside boat if the distance or places sacrificed to gain an inside overlap are excessive.

Asymmetric Leeward Mark

With a typical port-hand leeward mark, it generally pays to approach the mark on the starboard layline to gain as many inside overlaps as possible. In 'heavy traffic', more weight should be given to this guideline, even potentially above pressure and shifts.

So in the later stages of the run you should be seeking to position yourself to the left of your opposition so you have the best chance of owning the starboard layline leeward mark approach.

However, if you are not sailing in a pack, pressure and shifts should dictate your approach to the mark.

You need to be mindful of being 'boxed in' on the layline in an asymmetric if you aren't in the leading pack. In this situation, you are going to have to eat dirty air and confused waters for a long time which is painful and slow.

Forward planning is needed to avoid this.

You should aim to gybe before the pack to avoid becoming part of the pack. Aim to create as wide a lane as possible but be aware of how this may affect your leeward mark approach and rights.

As ever, these are guidelines. Shifts and especially pressure are king downwind and can drive you significantly away from these guidelines to make gains.

Leeward Gate

Just as for a leeward mark, your leeward gate plan should revolve around your exit plan.

Which mark you choose depends on:

- Next beat plan: This is usually the main factor determining which leeward gate to round. After the leeward gate, you will probably have to stay on the tack you round on for some time before you find clear wind, especially in a big fleet. So your choice of leeward gate largely determines your route up the first half of the next beat. If one side of the course is paying significantly, it can pay to sail more distance to the 'wrong' leeward gate to quickly head to the favoured side of the course, especially in traffic.

- How other boats are approaching the gate: If it is looking likely that you will be forced to round on the outside on one mark then it can pay to

Leeward Mark

Approaching the leeward mark you want to be on the left of your opponent (looking downwind)

Leeward Mark

So go to the starboard layline

Leeward Mark

And approach on starboard, claiming mark room

switch to the other leeward mark.
- Gusts & pressure approaching the gate: If there is significantly more pressure towards one leeward mark, consider rounding this one even if it is slightly further to sail. This is especially important in light and gusty winds, when wind-generated speed differences are greatest. Typically, other factors do override this, especially if the marks are close together and the wind is fairly consistent.

In the lovely event that you have a clear lead, or are clear of other boats, you can pick your leeward gate.

Before the start, if the leeward gate is laid, you should check which mark is furthest upwind. The method for this is the same as checking line bias (i.e. sail between the 2 buoys and set your sails; head in the opposite direction leaving your sails in the same position: if you have to sheet in, you are heading to the more upwind mark and vice versa). Knowing which mark is furthest upwind can determine your leeward gate plan if you are in clear water or if the other factors are evenly balanced.

Rounding the gate furthest upwind gives a double reward as you sail less distance both downwind and upwind.

Which leeward mark is furthest upwind may have changed if the wind has shifted. But remember that a boat length gained on leeward gate bias can be quickly more than lost if you end up rounding the mark which takes you to the wrong side of the race track.

When sailing downwind, it is often hard to call which leeward mark is furthest upwind. If you are unsure which is furthest upwind and there is no strategic preference on which one you should round, then leave your options open as long as possible by staying outside the layline for both marks.

You can then choose which leeward mark to round when you are much nearer the gate, making it easier to spot which one is nearest. In a fast boat or a yacht with a large crew, this may not work as

you need more time to prepare your leeward mark decision.

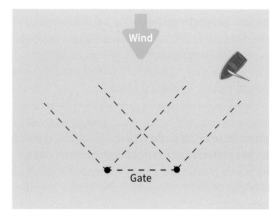

In this position, blue is pretty committed to the right-hand gate (looking downwind)

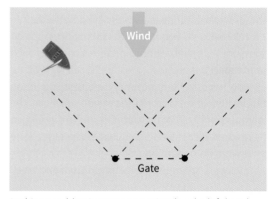

In this case, blue is pretty committed to the left-hand gate (looking downwind)

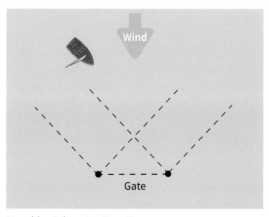

Here blue is keeping its options open

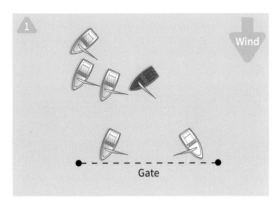

If the right-hand gate (looking downwind) is favoured, there may be heavy traffic

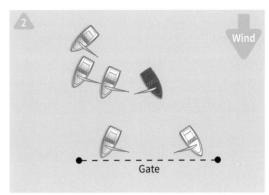

Blue may consider gybing and going for the left-hand gate (looking downwind)

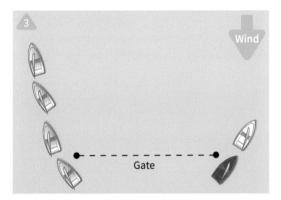

But this could leave blue exposed on the wrong side of the beat

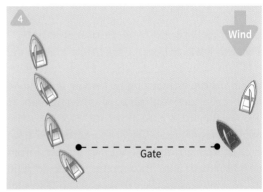

So, ideally, you would do a consolidating tack immediatley after rounding the mark

Before the race even starts, you should have a plan A on which leeward gate you will take. That helps as, in the heat of the battle of the race, it is good to have plan A in your head. As you sail the race, you should overlay any new information on your plan A and see if it has changed. Then, early on in the run, you need to be planning your approach to the correct leeward gate. This is the decision on the race course that you have to plan most in advance for.

If your plan goes awry and you are caught outside a boat or several boats, a late switch to the other leeward mark can be worthwhile. It is worth having in your head how much you will lose from switching to the less favoured mark so you know if a switch is worth making. Communication with your crew is key to making a switch work.

The exit from the leeward gate creates a lot of separation between boats so there is lot of scope for gains and losses. If you are sailing a conservative series you should look to consolidate your position as soon as possible. You need to be aware of how the fleet is spread between the gates and quickly look to tack or sail high / low to regain control of the fleet and your position.

Asymmetric Leeward Gate

Your exit plan is even more important for a leeward gate in an asymmetric because the fleet spreads out even more on the run than in symmetric boats or single-handers due to the bigger gybing angles. So your choice of leeward mark commits you for even longer to the tack you round on as the span of dirty wind and water is wider asymmetrics downwind.

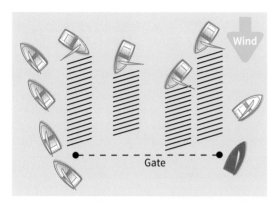

In an asymmetric there is usually a lot of dirty wind from the boats still on the run, so you are committed to the side you chose for longer

You also have as many rights coming in at speed on port at a starboard-hand leeward gate mark as you are the inside boat. However, a lot of people aren't aware of this so ensure your communication is clear. Be ready to back-out and protest if need be if your move is going to create a major incident.

With a late spinnaker drop, you can take a lot of places when you are down the fleet with this approach. It needs to be planned some way out and the layline picked well to ensure that you can come in with pace without overlaying the mark or underlaying and missing the 3-boat-length circle.

If you do underlay the mark or a windshift / pressure drop drags you high, it is often worth a double gybe to line up on the layline again. This re-establishes the powerful approach on starboard within 3 boat lengths. Of course some boats double gybe better than others so this needs to be considered.

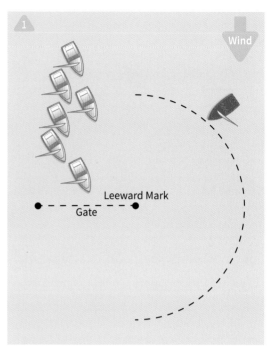

As already discussed, coming in on the starboard layline is what you should typically be aiming for

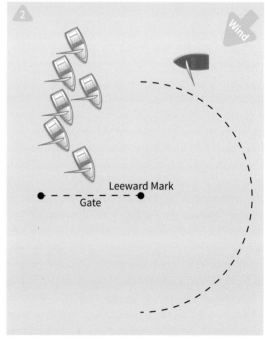

If a windshift (or less pressure) means that you won't get an overlap...

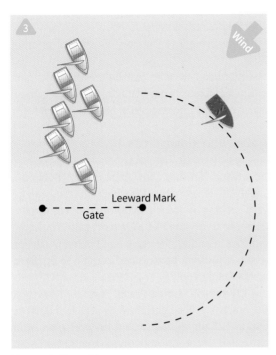

You are better gybing

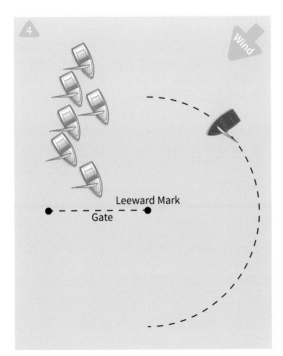

And then gybing back when you will have an overlap in the 3-boat-length circle

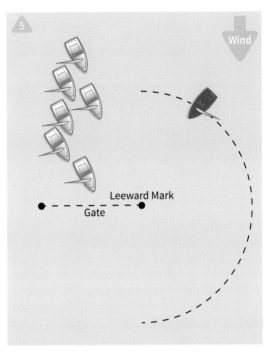

If the wind shifts back, you will be a double winner!

Upwind Finish Lines

Understanding the bias of the finish line shapes your finishing plan. Bias can be hard to assess from a distance so you should seek to stay away from both laylines to the finish for as long as possible to keep your options open. The more you stare at finish lines and attempt to assess bias from a distance (not easy!), the better you will get at it. One indicator is the angle of any flags on or near the finish line. If the back end of the flags are angling towards one end of the line, then that is the favoured end.

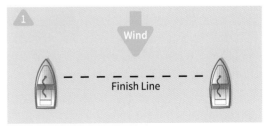

If the flags are pointing straight down the beat, there isn't a wind bias (although there may be a distance bias)

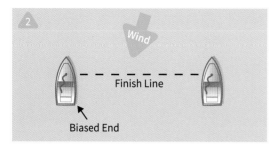

Biased End

But if the flags are angled toward one end of the line, then that is the favoured end (assuming there is no difference in distance)

If you are close behind an opponent and there is a safe gap to the next boat, you should seek to split ends (i.e. finish at the opposite end of the finish line to the boat in front) unless you think that you can out tack them or take a sneaky shift past them in the last few yards. If you split ends, you should aim to finish right at the end of the line to leverage as much line bias as possible to maximise the potential distance gain.

Occasionally a finish line is laid before the start or is shared with the start line. In this case, it is worth spending time understanding the finish line bias. If the finish line is shared with the start line, the finish line bias is opposite to the start line. You should allow for any windshifts since the start in your line-bias assessment.

If you have a really close finish with another boat, it can pay to use your momentum to luff towards head to wind just before the finish line to briefly increase your VMG. This can also gain an occasionally useful second in handicap racing.

Downwind Finish Lines

Downwind finishes are increasingly common, especially in asymmetric racing, and they can be very exciting. If you finish on the run, you should treat the finish line like a leeward gate. The same benefits of finding the mark / end of the finish line which is furthest upwind and coming in at speed on the inside apply.

If the finish is on a reach, consider how tight the reach is. If it is tight, the only attack or defence option is high so this should be your plan. Your approach to the previous mark should be based around the need to gain an inside overlap and sail high straight after the mark. On a broader reach, an overtaking lane below the boat in front, or the pack, may be possible, especially if the leeward finish end is biased. This can pay especially when the fleet push each other high and sail a 'bendy banana'.

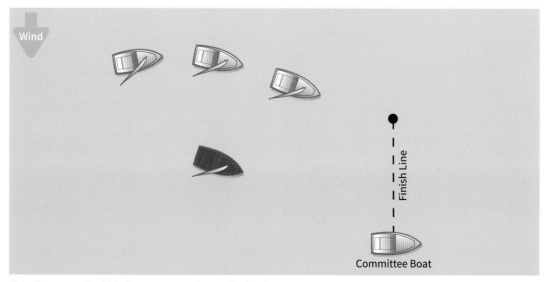

If the fleet are going high, it can pay to go low to the finish

CHAPTER 6

Fleet Tactics

It has been said many times that boatspeed is the magic ingredient that makes a good tactician. So true! Being able to turn on boatspeed at different angles fully opens up your tactical options (i.e. being able to sail fast in both high and low mode upwind and at different angles downwind).

Even without boatspeed, which disappears from everyone's armoury some days, you can still dig out results that count to keep momentum in your series through:

- Punchy starts
- Searching for wide lanes to accommodate your lack of pace
- Using the defensive tactics described in this book

Wind Shadows

Using your wind shadow is a key tactical weapon. Shadowing another boat's wind not only slows them down but, more importantly, distorts the wind. So your poor opponent won't be able to generate decent flow over their sails and so will be slower (and lower upwind).

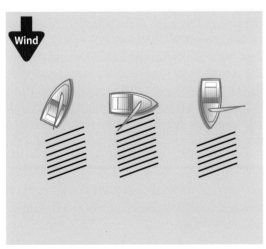

Typical wind shadows on the beat, reach and run

The upwind wind shadow varies significantly by boat depending on how much the wind bends over your sails. Knowing where wind shadows fall for your class of boat is very important for

understanding lanes. If you move to a new class, one of the first things to work out is where the wind shadows fall and the impact on lanes as this has a major influence on your tactical positioning.

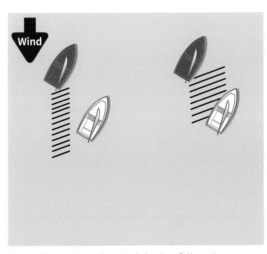

Depending on how the wind shadow falls in the particular class yellow may have a clear lane or have its wind disrupted significantly

These wind shadows determine where clear lanes are. A lane is a patch of water where you are in clear wind and water so are much more likely to be able to sail in the groove: i.e. high and fast.

Since dirty wind is disturbed as well as slowed,

in it you will struggle to maintain flow over the sails. This makes sailing smoothly challenging and it becomes nearly impossible to keep the boat in the groove. So upwind, you will lose height as well as speed. On runs, you will lose depth as well as speed. Avoid dirty wind if possible!

If your opposition are considerate enough to use a burgee, that is a useful guide for where their wind shadow is.

Awareness of wind shadows and lanes should ideally become so drilled in that this becomes second nature. So the thought of trying to leebow someone in a B14 or hold a lane just to windward and behind someone in an OK wouldn't cross your mind as you know these are untenable situations.

The Leebow

This can be a very effective tool for pushing an opponent to the wrong side of the course and reducing the loss of distance from ducking another boat's stern. However, it is rare that the right place to tack is where an opponent happens to be. So your default position is typically to duck an opponent as you have presumably chosen the tack you are on for a good reason!

If you were looking to tack anyway or a shift / pressure happens to arrive so it is the right time to tack, then a leebow tack may be appropriate. Keep in mind that an aggressive leebow tack, especially early in a race, may annoy your opposition for which you may receive payback!

Tactics Mode

You should always be consciously sailing in attack, consolidate or defend mode. If you're not sure what mode you are in, it is likely that your tactics will be aimless, potentially resulting in major unplanned place losses and an inconsistent series.

Which mode you choose to sail in depends on where you are versus your objective and, critically, how the fleet is distributed around you. So, if you have a pack close behind, you would typically sail more defensively. If you have a pack ahead and a big gap behind, you would typically sail more offensively (attack mode, not swearing as you sail!).

Upwind

Attacking

Focusing forward is the way to attack a race upwind. You should not be looking backwards at your opposition or you risk missing windshifts or gusts coming down the race track. You should be solely focused on the gust and shift pattern ahead and attacking each shift by following your instincts and tacking as soon as it feels right to do so. Trust your instincts and make fast decisions. If you have put the time in, they will generally be right. The more time you put in sailing in quality fleets, the more accurate your instincts become.

To make this work, you need excellent boat handling and good pace without needing to stare at your telltales (covered in *Helming to Win*). Your focus should only be on the pressure and shifts ahead. You can ignore other boats because, if you are in phase, you will be moving forward and so don't need to worry about where the opposition is. Not being distracted by other boats or what has just happened is critical for entering and staying in this attacking mode.

However, this is high risk because, if you lose phase with the gusts and shifts, you could well expose yourself as you haven't been watching the fleet. But this is the fastest way to move forward in a race when this level of risk is appropriate. This risk can be appropriate if you need a top result in a race and you are behind your objective. But it can also be appropriate if you have a big gap behind so can move into hard attack mode for a period.

When a sailor or team of sailors is in phase, defence is challenging because your opposition can only sail the gusts and shifts as well as this if they also solely focus forward, which is hard to do when defending.

Consolidating

Upwind consolidating is often achieved by covering the opposition.

You need to know the lanes for your boat: when your wind is clear from the boats below (i.e. not being leebowed) and above (i.e. not in their wind

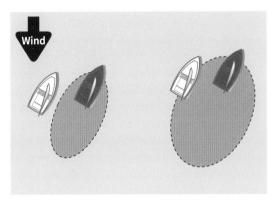

Depending on how the wind shadow falls in the particular class yellow may be being leebowed or may not

shadow). These vary significantly by boat, so lanes can look very different.

You should know the leebow position for your boat and know the sure cover position. As you make these moves or become exposed to them, you should also be aware of how quickly these positions will be lost if windshifts change the angles of the boats or your opponent makes distance in a gust. This will help with your positioning to keep your leebow or sure cover for longer.

Ideally, your positioning should include the expected impact of upcoming shifts. This isn't easy and requires being in the rhythm of the wind pattern.

On windier days, if it is late in a race and there is no pressure for your position, it is a good time to rest, especially if tomorrow is looking like another day of hard work.

Controlling the race is easier in more stable (consistent strength), steadier (consistent direction) winds. Most typically these conditions are in a force 4+ on the sea with the wind blowing from the sea.

Controlling a race is harder in less stable, shiftier conditions. Typically these are experienced inland, when the wind is blowing offshore over large obstacles or in warm thermal sea breezes.

Each type of wind requires a different approach to consolidating.

In stable, steady conditions, controlling a race is much easier and recovery from a poor start much harder. If you are ahead, you can control a race by shepherding the fleet towards the middle of the course so they are easier to cover. 'Shepherding' involves covering boats who are splitting from the pack hard to encourage them to tack back. You should cover boats sailing towards the pack loosely to encourage them to carry on.

What appears to be a safe cover

Can be lost through a windshift

If this windshift was anticipated, blue should have sailed higher to get more space between them

So when the windshift came, the cover was maintained

If yellow is threatening to break away from the pack, a tight cover may encourage them to go back with the pack

On the other hand, if they are sailing back to the pack, a loose cover is more appropriate

Of course, as with all tactics, you need to do this whilst keeping half an eye on shifts and pressure. If you need to protect a lead for some time, a loose cover is more appropriate. When you aren't sure if you are going the right way, you should cover more tightly. If you are pretty sure you are going the right way, you can ease up your cover and even let your opposition split a bit to take a gain.

In less stable, shiftier conditions, if you try to control the fleet you will drop backwards through it. You need to stay in phase with the windshifts and pressure which is unlikely if you are tightly covering boats because they are probably sailing in different wind.

In these conditions, you should continue to attack the shifts and pressure while keeping half an eye on where the fleet is. A good crew can

really help with this by allowing the helm to stay in phase with the wind while the fine crew shares information about positioning against the fleet

You should seek to stick with the majority of the fleet to consolidate. Later in the race, you may have room to sacrifice some distance if there is a gap before the next boat so you can cover harder.

It is rare for the wind to be completely stable, so consolidating usually means continuing to play the shifts and pressure to some degree, while keeping an eye on the fleet.

In summary, put more emphasis on covering the fleet in more stable winds and more focus on shifts / pressure in more unstable breeze.

Defending

'Golden positioning' for upwind defence is to position yourself between the fleet / your key opponent and the windward mark. This means that, no matter which way the wind shifts, you are well protected.

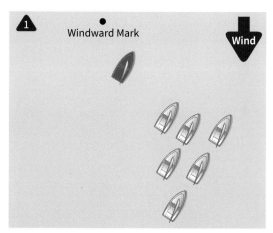

When defending, stay between the fleet and the windward mark

As doing it will lose you distance, you should use tight defence or attack hard only when appropriate:

- Late in a race
- When you are solely focused on one opponent
- When there is a significant gap to the next group of boats

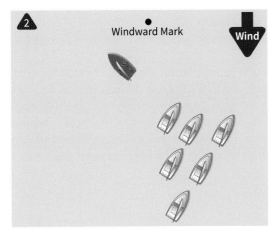

Don't go off on a limb – it is a high risk which you don't need to take

In a very close tacking match, watch out for your mast clipping the boat to leeward as you roll tack.

Reaches

Attacking
The most effective attack on a reach is generally high of the pack in clear water.

Wake from other boats can flatten nice waves up to a couple of boat lengths to windward. Getting into time and rhythm with the waves is critical for downwind speed and not at all easy. It is much harder to do when wave patterns are disturbed by other boats. Also, if you can steer over the waves freely with potentially big changes in angles, you will be faster than if you are constrained by having to steer round other boats.

Being able to sail reasonably fast in disturbed water is as important a skill as being able to sail well in dirty wind.

" Following in the footsteps of the great Laser sailors, I've spent many hours training in the Solent. The tricky, choppy waves in the Solent are great practice for sailing in disturbed water. If you can make a rhythm out of the Solent waves, you can find that rhythm anywhere.

However, in the build-up to the 2017 OK Worlds in Barbados, I spent more time in Christchurch Bay where the waves are longer and rolling, similar to Barbados (apart from the temperature and absence of white sand!). "

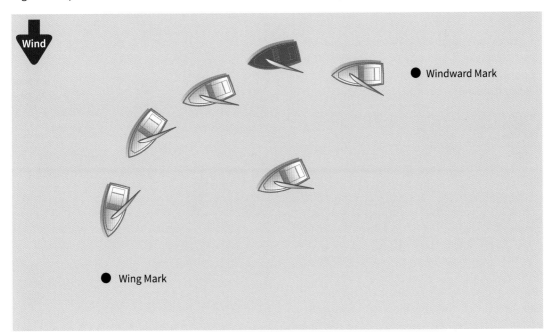

Attacking on a reach usually involves going high of the pack in clear water

This means that a clear attacking lane is often a couple of lengths to windward of the main pack. An early, punchy move high just after the windward mark is usually the best way to find this lane. Ideally with an element of surprise! In a spinnaker boat, this may mean a late hoist. Sailing only just high of the pack will typically lead to a reaction in the form of a luff. This means sailing more distance but without creating a lane of clear water from which to attack.

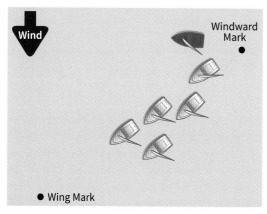

Going high just after the windward mark is a useful; attacking move on the reach

To attack one boat on a reach, you should go just to windward and out of their wake. If your opponent misses a wave and you don't, you will quickly blanket their wind and overtake.

To attack one boat, go just to windward, out of their wake

The power of this positioning to attack an opponent creates the 'banana' above the rhumb line on the 1st reach (as seen on p41).

Hard Attack

If you cannot overtake the opponent you need to pass, a radical attack is to keep attacking high and allow yourself to be luffed so eventually the reach turns into a run. A run is the easiest point of sailing from which to attack when behind. You will lose a lot of distance initially so this should be used only in rare circumstances when major distance losses are a good trade-off for a single place gain.

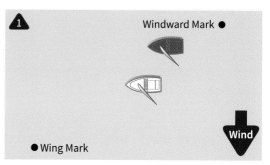

If it is just one boat that matters, and you can't get past, encourage them to luff you...

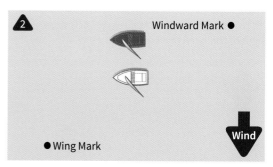

Keep going high...

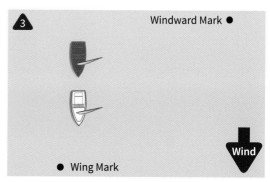

So you end up on a run down to the mark – much easier to overtake

Consolidating

In most situations, you should protect your windward side but be mindful of the distance losses from doing that. If you are confident with your speed, you should take any opportunity to find a low lane and let the pack sail the extra distance of the 'high banana'.

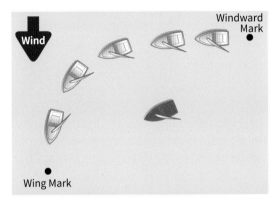

If the whole fleet is going high, going low can be a consolidating move

If you can, encourage others around you to make the right choice and head down the rhumb line so gaining distance for everyone.

Only on a very broad reach, especially with tide pushing you to windward, should your priority switch to protecting your leeward side. Also, late on the first reach, you should protect your leeward side to prevent anyone gaining an overlap.

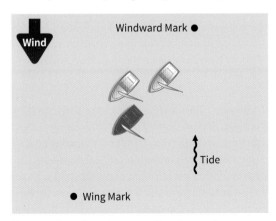

On a very broad reach, or near the wing mark, you should look to protect your leeward side

Defending

To defend hard against an opponent, you need to demonstrate your intentions early with a sharp luff. It pays to have a reputation as a 'luffer'. So at training events, it is worth making a point of never letting boats pass to windward so people know it's not a route that's even worth trying. Some lost places at training events are worthwhile to enhance your reputation as a luffer – you can buy the poor windward boat a beer later!

Symmetric Runs

Attacking

This is a great place to attack as you can control your opponent and effectively blanket their wind. You can slow your opponent considerably, so closing distance. However, actually overtaking is harder, unless you have great boatspeed, so you should aim to draw your opponent in through blanketing their wind and then aiming for the side which will give you an inside overlap at the next mark. If you are still a long way from the leeward mark, you should attack the side which gives best wind and waves.

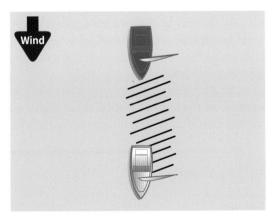

Downwind it is easy to attack and slow the opposition down

To actually overtake, you sometimes need to separate from your opponent to find clear water and waves. When attacking a pack, it often pays to split from the pack to find clear wind and waves.

To attack a pack of boats, separate from them, looking for clear wind and waves

Packs of boats are generally slow downwind as the disturbance to each other's wind and, critically, waves is considerable.

Despite these attacking techniques downwind being appropriate sometimes, it is important to remember that blanketing an opponent and working for the inside overlap can mean lost distance and lost focus on wind and waves. So if you are attacking a group, it often pays to attack by sailing fast and focusing on the best wind and waves rather than blanketing boats. If you can sail fast in good waves and wind and blanket some of the pack you are chasing, that is the perfect world.

As with all the tactical guidelines in this book, pressure and shifts are key and often overrule the 'textbook manoeuvres'.

In attack mode, you should focus forward, just as you would upwind in attack mode. To focus on moving forward, you should be looking back for pressure and forward for the best route through waves. So very much head out of the boat mode! And a potentially sore neck!!

Defence

You can use your opponent's burgee to indicate where their dirty wind lane is. Another reason not to use a burgee!

Being ahead on a run is the hardest position to defend. If you are defending against a pack of boats, look to keep a lane of clear air. Being ahead on a run requires similar tactics as for being behind

upwind. Just as when you are behind upwind, you are ideally looking for clear wind lanes without sailing to the corners.

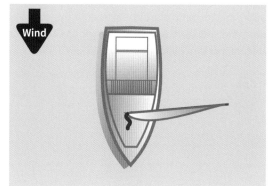

Use your opponent's burgee to see where their wind shadow will lie

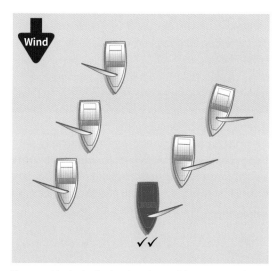

You need to try to find a clear lane without separating from the pack

If you can't find a clear wind lane then splitting from the pack is usually better than being sucked into the pack in dirty air. This can feel uncomfortable if you have a well drilled-in tactical conservatism. How much you need to split depends on how much dirty wind you think you are going to have to chew by sticking with the pack. Dirty wind has a greater effect in light winds, so clear lanes are most critical in light winds and less so when it is windy.

Asymmetric Runs

Attacking

You should avoid the pack, or groups of boats, to sail in as clear wind and waves as possible. This is the one time in a race where you should be very comfortable and keen to split from the pack. In doing this, you should be 'attacking the pressure' (i.e. staying in as much wind as possible and gybing back across pressure to re-use it).

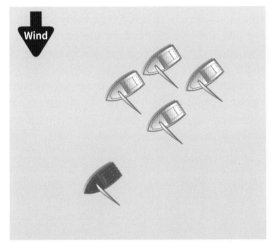

Attack the pressure and make sure you are in clear wind and waves

If you find yourself gybing and sailing into no pressure, quickly assess where the next pressure is. Often a gybe straight back pays as that should put you back in the pressure you were just enjoying (see p51).

Pressure generally rules over windshifts in asymmetrics downwind but in shifty winds, angles can matter more. I would not usually use a compass downwind to spot windshifts as the big ones should be clear from the angles of other boats and your angle versus the leeward marks. If you are staring at your compass, you are probably losing the pressure picture downwind which is highly dynamic and so needs watching and re-assessing as much as possible. Being able to sail with your head out of the boat (covered in *Helming to Win*) is a key enabler of this.

Consolidating

If you round the windward mark with a boat or pack behind that you need to beat, you should seek to soak low as early as possible so you achieve golden positioning (i.e. placing your boat between your opposition and the next mark). In doing this, you should be careful not to drop so far to leeward so that you put yourself in or at risk of dirty wind if there is a lift or pressure increase from above.

Soak low when you can

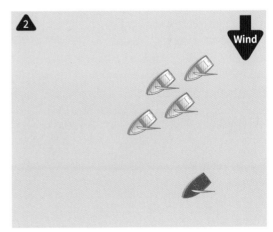

But don't soak so low that you are in danger of being in dirty wind

With asymmetric downwind sailing, attack is often best form of defence. It pays to keep attacking pressure and shifts when you are only seeking to consolidate whilst keeping an eye on where the fleet is. You should seek gusts and shifts to stay in the same zone as the fleet without being covered from behind. If you try too hard to consolidate (rather than attack), you typically sink down the fleet fast in an asymmetric downwind.

Defence

This is a hard leg of the course to sail defensively. Controlled attack is often the best form of defence. As for consolidating, keep attacking the shifts and pressure but keep an even closer eye on the fleet. Be prepared to swallow some distance losses to stay with the fleet or your key opponents.

If the wind is particularly unstable (i.e. big pressure differences and little substance to the gusts – typical warm weather, patchy sea breeze conditions), then you may choose to attack more outright and stay more focused on pressure and watch the fleet very little.

Hard Defence

When all you need to do is hold a place and you have some distance to burn, you should stay between your opponent and the next mark (or finish line). Keep your bow out on the long gybe.

If your opponent is sailing well, hard defence will lose distance fairly quickly as it will put you out of phase with the shifts / pressure if your opponent is in phase. So you should only use hard defence when appropriate (e.g. for the last few gybes into the finish line to protect a position). If you defend hard too early, you risk being blanketed and overtaken. If you defend hard too late, you risk your opponent sailing past you in a 'lucky' gust or shift!

If you have a big lead, you can defend hard earlier. If you find your lead rapidly disappearing, you need to change modes quickly back to consolidate or even attack mode.

CHAPTER 7

Boat-on-Boat Tactics

Knowing your opposition is important. Some sailors are relatively passive and some more aggressive. You can be more confident of overtaking moves working against passive opponents so you should be more ready to try an overtaking move. With an aggressive opponent, you need to ensure that you have a clear overtaking opportunity before making a move or you are likely to end up wasting distance through a luffing match or similar. You should also leave a bit more space to avoid an unnecessary incident.

Upwind

Attacking

If you are sailing in a pack or group of boats, you should aim to find shifts or pressure that move you into anti-phase with the pack around you so you are sailing in clearer pressure. Other boats' sails generate a lot of dirty wind and wind likes to bend past obstacles. So you will advance even if the shifts / pressure you take are average because you will have clearer air than the other boats. On the sea, splitting will mean you sail in more consistent waves which are easier to steer in an effective rhythm.

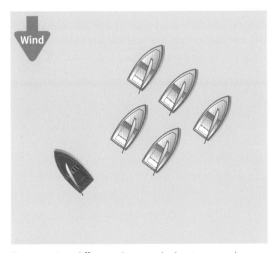

Try to get in a different phase to the boats around you

If it is late in the race and you have a few boats to potentially attack with no risk of being overtaken, you should throw in lots of tacks or gybes in the hope of forcing an error from your opposition. Good boat handling helps. If you are very close to your opponent, but they are covering well, you can try a dummy tack to split with them whilst on a good windshift / pressure.

You should aim simultaneously to attack and defend by loose covering the boats behind whilst splitting with those in front, ideally on a decent shift or pressure.

You should seek to leverage starboard advantage. To overtake someone on port you need to be a boat length clear. To catch another boat up on starboard, you only need to be within a boat length. So planning your final approach on starboard can be almost a 2-boat-length gain in tactical advantage. In close situations, or late in a leg, you should aim to get on the right hand side of your opponent so that you end up with the starboard tack advantage. As ever, picking a good shift or decent pressure is a more effective way to overtake than this.

When attacking, you can 'put the hammer down' in moderate or windy weather to find an extra burst of speed just when it is needed (e.g. a marginal leebow), trying to roll someone to force them to tack. You should hike and work the sails extra hard for perhaps a 10 second burst. This work rate will be harder than your opposition unless they are doing the same thing at the same time, which is rare. Of course, you should use this tool judiciously as you don't want to end up drained for the rest of the race.

The leebow tack can be a very powerful tool when things get close. The real power of the move is forcing your opponent to tack onto the unfavoured tack. Being in phase with the shifts and pressure is vital for that so you know when it is right to go for a leebow tack and when it is better to take a duck.

As you approach an opponent what do you do?

If you are expecting a lift, stay on port (the favoured tack), ducking if necessary

But if you are expecting a header, you should leebow on starboard (the favoured tack) and hopefully force your opponent off on port (the unfavoured tack)

How close you can legally tack to another boat's leebow varies greatly by boat (e.g. an Enterprise tacks very quickly so you can tuck in close to an opponent). However, a leebow tack is very hard to pull off in a B14 which has wings, moves fast through the water and is slow to tack. Close-quarter 2-boat tuning is a great way to learn where the 'point of death' is with a leebow (i.e. the place where you can no longer live with being leebowed and you quickly slow up or slip sideways).

The leebow position varies significantly by class. The leebow position is when you kill the lane for the windward boat so they either slip to leeward into your wind shadow completely or can only stay to windward of you through excessive pinching, resulting in a loss of speed.

The leebow effect works via the wind exiting your sails at a tighter angle than they enter your sails as your sails work as an aerofoil. This angle change varies by boat so the effectiveness of a leebow tack varies by boat. Also, some boats can handle a leebow situation better than others depending on how well the rigs eat dirt and how well the foils work. So, for example: a Merlin Rocket is very hard to leebow; an OK relatively easy (see p68).

Consolidating

To consolidate your position you should continue to sail for shifts and pressure but keep an eye on your opposition. So you may sail through a shift (i.e. not tack on what you think is a header), if that keep you in touch with your opposition

If yellow decides not to tack on a header you may also choose not to and stay with him

If the wind is shifty and unstable, spending too much time looking at the opposition and following their track will cause you to lose phase with windshifts and pressure. In these conditions, your cover needs to be looser and you need to be less distracted by the fleet or your attempt to consolidate will result in place losses.

In steadier wind, you can afford to cover harder and watch the fleet more to ensure that you consolidate your position.

As this cover becomes more instinctive, the difference between your attack and consolidate mode can reduce which makes both modes more effective. So ideally, you can continue to attack shifts and pressure effectively whilst also keeping half an eye on where the fleet is.

Defending

How hard you defend a position depends on how far advanced the race is, how the fleet is distributed and where you are versus your outcome objectives.

Progression of race: Early in a race, defending hard would be a gamble except in extreme circumstances (e.g. you just need to stop one opponent to win a championship). Defending hard early in a race could result in place losses that you are unable to make up. At this stage the fleet is much more tightly compacted so any distance loss from being involved with other boats can result in a lot of places lost. Therefore you should usually focus on your own race early in the race and avoid boat-on-boat tactical battles.

Fleet distribution: If there is a big gap in front of you and a big gap after the boat you are defending against, a hard defence may make sense as you aren't potentially foregoing place gains or risking place losses. This works the other way – hard attack can be appropriate if there is a big gap behind you and lots of opportunity for gain ahead.

Status vs. outcome objective: If you are ahead of your objectives and this place is key you may choose to defend hard. If you are behind your objectives, you should probably be attacking the race rather than defending.

Defending hard upwind means staying between your opposition and the windward mark and sitting on their wind to ensure that they receive dirty wind so slowing them up.

However, it can be appropriate to increase the gap on the boat behind (e.g. you are about to head onto a downwind leg to the finish where an increased gap greatly reduces your vulnerability to attack). In this case you need to stop defending and start attacking.

If your opponent is getting very close to you and may slip by, things may get too close to keep defending hard and, again, attack may be your best option.

> At the 1989 Bloody Mary (yes, it appears that I am old!), we were lying 3rd up the final beat in a Cadet with Rob Larke very close behind us. There was no scope for place gains. So we covered Rob hard. Rob overtook us because he stayed in phase with the shifts whilst we tried to cover. It did not work as we were always out of phase with the shifts and got sucked backwards. An early lesson on when to stop defending hard!

In these circumstances, you should aim to move back into attack mode, working the shifts and pressure to stay ahead and, if possible, protect the right-hand side. If things are close, the starboard boat has right of way. However, you should be fluid on this. If left is paying heavily, you should protect left.

Reaches

Attacking

On the reach, attacking to windward is typically the fastest way to gain places.

The exceptions to this are on a very broad leg or late on the first reach, when it can often pay to attack an opponent to leeward as you approach the gybe mark. To overtake your opponent to leeward, you just need an overlap whereas to overtake to windward you need to break clear ahead. So overtaking to leeward is a boat length easier than overtaking to windward as you approach the mark rounding.

However, gaining and holding an overlap is much harder on a tighter angle as you will be trying to hold that overlap in dirty air. So, on a tight reach, you should usually aim to overtake to windward.

Nevertheless, late in the leg, it can pay to seek an inside overlap rather than trying to pass to windward. With good timing you can establish an overlap to leeward fairly late and aim to just hold it for the few boat lengths into the mark.

If there is no issue with losing some distance (e.g. big gap on the boat behind and you don't need to catch the boats in front to achieve your outcome objectives) and you don't think you will manage a windward pass, you should aim to overlap to leeward early and take your opponent as high as is legitimate.

As leeward boat, you are entitled to sail your proper course. A high route can be justified if there is more wind or better waves to windward. An expected upcoming windshift may also justify sailing high. By sailing yourself and your opponent high, the final approach to the gybe mark will be broader which increases your chances of gaining water.

Consolidating

To consolidate your position, you should protect your windward side, so you aren't rolled, but dive low towards the rhumb line when there aren't boats attacking you to windward.

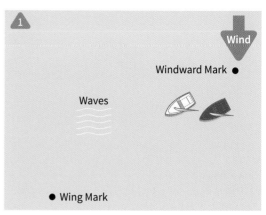

If you can't overtake to windward, but there is a reason to sail high (e.g. better waves), establish an overlap to leeward

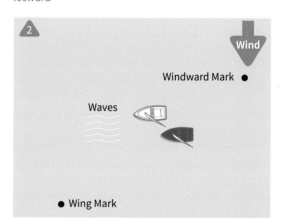

And sail your proper course to the waves, forcing yellow high

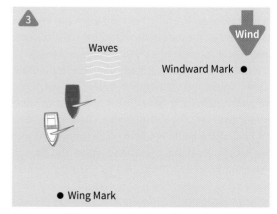

Then you will have to run down to the mark and it is much easier to attack and get room at the mark

How hard you protect to windward depends on how tight the reach is and how much boats to windward slow you in your particular class. They always do, but how much varies (e.g. in a Merlin Rocket losing your lane to windward on anything but a very broad reach is death; in a single-hander in waves, the cost is low if you still have just enough space to keep working the waves effectively).

Defending

The best defence is usually to hold a high lane. Whilst this is effective in stopping boats overtaking, it can result in distance losses to those ahead and add to the first reach 'banana' (see p41). So ideally, you will defend your lane while going high by as little as you can get away with.

To defend against someone trying to establish a late, leeward inside overlap (see above), you should push as low as possible late in the leg (see p59).

Symmetric Runs

Attacking

To attack one boat, you should aim to blanket their wind. This makes playing the spinnaker for your opponent hard as the wind is disturbed. The wind for your opponent is also slowed so you will quickly close up (see p73). This is an aggressive tactic so should be deployed judiciously.

To escape your dirty wind, your opponent has to sail more distance than you, so you gain every time they try to escape your dirt. Your opponent may try to gybe. You should look for the signs of that (e.g. crew getting ready to release poles, tiller extension going behind the helm etc.). That will enable you to anticipate their move and stick on their wind.

If you time your gybes and steering back on to your opponent's dirty wind with windshifts and greater pressure you can make further gains.

In a tight boat-on-boat situation, a double gybe is a punchy move but a great way to gain luffing rights. If you double gybe, you are on a new gybe so you regain luffing rights until the windward

boat has managed to break clear ahead again. A double gybe can be pulled off very quickly with a small turn and a flick of the boom across your head.

Consolidating

This is a hard leg to consolidate on. Similarly to any other run, you are looking to sail fast in the right direction whilst keeping clear air and managing risk. These goals are often incompatible. It is usually better to keep clear air via a little separation from the fleet so taking some can reduce risk rather than sit in dirty air in the pack.

Defence

To defend against a boat attacking you directly, you should seek to keep sailing fast in pressure and favourable shifts. If you find a shift or pressure to escape the cover whilst not sailing too much extra distance then take these opportunities. The best defence is not being in your opponent's dirty air so slightly forward or back from that depending on which side of the course is critical to defend.

If you are covering your opposition they will look for ways to get clear wind

If they gybe, gybe with them and ensure you are still blanketing them

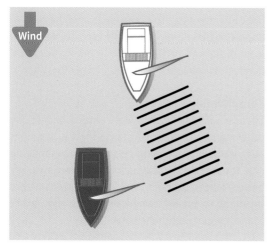

To defend against attack try to position yourself slightly away from their wind shadow

If someone is really intent on sitting on your wind, they will gain and catch you eventually. However, defending against someone really keen on overtaking you is possible. With appropriate defence, you should become very hard to overtake but you will lose distance in your defence. So you need to balance up how important this one place is to you versus managing the fleet. This depends on your position versus your outcome goals, how your opponent affects your goals and how advanced the race is.

To defend early / mid-way down the run, protect the favoured side of the course. So it is important to have a good idea which side is favoured. Later in the run, protect your inside overlap.

" *In race 6 of the 2017 Merlin Rocket Nationals, we led at the last windward mark by a few boat lengths from Andy 'Taxi' Davis & Alex Warren with just a run to the finish. We put ourselves between Taxi & Alex and the leeward mark and they gradually closed us in by smothering our wind (and sailing the waves well!). In hindsight, we should have put on a loose cover, positioning ourselves slightly more out to sea than a tight cover to take advantage of the nicer waves out there. Our tight cover allowed Taxi & Alex to close level with us going into the finish. We aimed to sail them past the starboard layline in order to give them dirty wind and stay ahead*

even if they got their noses out. On the last wave before performing our winning move they caught a lovely (for them) wave, gained a length and gybed round the front of us. A tight cover on a run should only be performed late in the race with a decent lead, not from the start of the run with a few lengths' lead. "

Asymmetric Runs

Attacking

As for upwind, you will sail fastest when you have your head out of the boat and are attacking every gust and shift. This is potentially risky as such intense focus on pressure and shifts means that you can lose sight of the fleet and so take risks. A good crew can help massively in observing the other boats and feeding the helm relevant information. Developing the skill of attacking the race whilst still being able to keep half an eye on the fleet also helps.

Consolidating

You should continue to attack the pressure and shifts or you will be sucked backwards. But to consolidate you should keep a keener eye on where the pack is. You should aim to position yourself between the pack and the leeward mark without losing your lane and remaining in good pressure (see p49).

This is not easy as the distribution of the pack changes much faster downwind in an asymmetric than upwind. So consolidating is challenging because, to keep an eye on such a dynamic fleet, you need to look at the fleet a lot which means running a high risk of losing the pressure / shift pattern.

Again, the more you practise doing this (by sailing as much as possible in large, competitive fleets), the easier it gets. If you are unsure what to do, bias towards attacking the shifts / pressure as losing sight of these always results in place losses.

Defending

This is the hardest defence to manage! Your positioning should ideally be between your opponent and the leeward mark, whilst protecting the starboard layline. However, you can't be dogmatic about this or you will lose sight of the pressure and shifts and a good opponent will soon pass you.

Defending one boat, or a chasing pack, hard will result in rapid distance loss. If you are in the final stages of a race, that can be an appropriate tactic. You need to judge how quickly you will lose distance and time your defence so you can just stay ahead. There are no bonus points for winning races by extra seconds so don't be afraid to give up distance to secure a win or any result that is worth defending given your outcome goals.

> " *In race 4 of the 2015 D-One Worlds, I rounded the first windward mark in 2nd place with a nice gap on the pack behind. I was leading the regatta*

and, as it stood, potentially extending my lead. All very nice! It had generally paid to stay on starboard gybe round the mark and head for the cliffs. So I focused on boatspeed to hunt down the lead. What I had not factored into my plan was that the wind was unstable and shifty.

That called for a conservative strategy. I should have worked very low or gybed to get between the fleet and the leeward mark. The pack rounded the windward mark in new pressure which then shifted left 40 degrees so most sailors gybed at the spreader mark onto the now long port gybe in pressure.

I got hammered for my earlier decision to attack the lead and not cover. 11 boats passed, so I dropped to 13th in a 2 lap race. Once I had let the wind gods know my dissatisfaction, I re-learnt the lesson of conservative big fleet sailing when you are ahead of your outcome objectives... again!"

Re-learning the lesson of being conservative when ahead of your outcome objectives

CHAPTER 8

Bringing It All Together

This book has covered many scenarios and options. Tactics are potentially complex. However, at your main events you shouldn't think too hard and trust your instincts. Just go with what feels right (i.e. go with your gut feel and invariably it will be the right decision if you have put the time in).

Your gut instinct is all your past experiences rolled into an instant thought so should be trusted!

> *The best leg I ever sailed was at the 2014 D-One Worlds on the penultimate run. I was 15th at the windward mark behind both my main rivals for the event. Under pressure, I reverted to gut instinct and just sailed the boat hard, attacking every wave and gybing for every bit of pressure completely forgetting where I was or the consequences if I stayed 15th. It was a dream run on which I went from 15th to 6th which was enough to win the event. It helped that I was between jobs so I had sailed the D-One nearly every day for a month so my speed and gut instincts were good.*

Teamwork

Teamwork is vital to good decision making. In a 2+ person boat, major tactical decisions should be made after some discussion. You should have a decision making framework so you don't debate decisions for too long under pressure (e.g. crew provides input, helm makes final decision or crew makes all decisions etc.). This framework should be based around the relative strengths of the helm and crew and also their view (e.g. in a trapeze boat, the crew has a better view of the wind than the helm, so may be better making strategic calls whilst the helm makes boat-on-boat tactical calls).

Not all decisions can be discussed. Some of the best decisions are made instinctively and quickly (e.g. reacting to windshifts and pressure on a shifty and gusty lake). The opportunity will have passed if each of these decisions is discussed.

Before the race, there is time to discuss the race plan in detail so that is always a good discussion to have. If you are sailing a single-hander, it can be useful to bounce your race plan off a tuning partner. Even if you are very confident in your plan, there may always be information you have missed.

Teamwork is vital to success

Race Review

After every race, you should review all tactical situations and think about how you might have come out in better shape. Talking this over with someone else can really help. Replay the tape of the race in your head and think about your moves and your opposition counter-moves. This will help build your tactical memory so your instincts become stronger with time.

Wrong decisions should only be discussed after the race and then with a positive mind-set on how future decisions can be improved, not seeking blame. Everyone makes wrong decisions. Your discussion should be focused on:

- Given the information you had at the time, was the decision right?
- With the information you have now, would you have made a different decision?

The latter is often the case. This new information might be about the venue in which case it should be built into your future decision making and venue notes.

The more that tactics become instinctive, the more your head is cleared to focus on getting into groove with the windshifts and pressure and sailing fast in a straight line. Tactics become instinctive from doing a lot of racing in high quality fleets. Take every opportunity you can to sail against best possible opposition in the biggest fleets.

At the 2012 Endeavour Trophy, we were soundly beaten by Ben Saxton & Alan Roberts who were both in their early 20s. By this age, they both had more big fleet experience sailing than me. I'd been racing at 5 - 10 Champs a year which is a lot of an amateur and has helped a lot over the years. However, these guys came from the top end of Optimists and youth sailing where the size and quality of the fleets mean that sailors can effectively be sailing in 30 big fleet events a year! They are also very talented and importantly have worked hard and constantly sought to improve.

Hopefully the most important thing you will take away from this final chapter is to ignore the preachings of this book if you are in the groove with the wind! At the big events, don't overcomplicate things and go with what your gut says will work.

Happy sailing!

Go with your gut instinct

RACING RULES

The Rules in Practice 2021-2024
Bryan Willis

INCLUDES THE NEW RULES IN FULL

Rules in Practice 2025-2029 will be published in late 2024

Fully updated for (and contains in full) the 2021-2024 Racing Rules of Sailing & features a brand new chapter on the luffing rules and how they are being applied.

When the windward mark is an obstruction

Could I hail for room to tack?

This situation occurs only when the mark is also an obstruction (other than a starting mark when approaching the line to start). The mark might be a large metal buoy or a boat (maybe displaying flag M, replacing the original mark that has drifted out of place).

You are A:
• Provided that you need to tack, and you are certain the other boat is not fetching the mark, you may hail to B for room to tack. 'Water' may be misunderstood; 'Room to tack' is best. (Rule 20.1)
• If B hails 'You tack' in response to your hail, and then ducks your stern or crosses safely ahead of you and fetches the mark, you have broken a rule (because you had no right to hail). If he is agrieved you must take a penalty, or he could protest you. If he responds to your hail by tacking, he might protest and claim in a protest hearing that he could have layed the mark, or that you could have easily sailed below the mark. (Rule 20.1)
• If you judge that B can get round the mark without passing head to wind, you are still the right-of-way boat provided you don't pass head to wind yourself. So even if you don't have luffing rights, you may go up to head to wind in order to 'shoot the mark', and B must keep clear. (Rule 11 & Definition Proper Course)
• For you to have the right to hail, you have to be close-hauled or above and on a course from which you must make a substantial change to avoid

the obstruction. If you were further to leeward, so that the obstruction was not in your path, then you would not have the right to hail; you would have to slow down and tack behind B or bear away and gybe. (Definition Obstruction)
• If you do hail for room to tack, you must tack as soon as there is room. You can't hail and then 'shoot the mark' by going head to wind and bearing away around the mark. (Rule 20.2(d))

You are B:
• As the windward boat you must keep clear if A luffs in an attempt to 'shoot the mark'. If he luffs as needed to shoot the mark he does not have to give you room to keep clear. (Rules 11 & 43.1(b))
• If A hails for room to tack, even if you are sure that you could get round the mark without tacking, you must respond to the hail (by tacking or hailing 'You tack'). You cannot just tell A that he has no right to hail for room to tack. (Rule 20.2(b))
• If A hails for room to tack, and you are not sure that you can get round the mark without tacking, then you must either tack or hail back 'You tack' and give room to A to tack. (Rules 20.2(b) & (c))

---

9. On the Reach

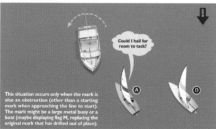

You are A:
• You are the right-of-way boat and you may change course as you please. (Rule 12)

You are B:
• Your only obligation is to keep clear of A (because you are clear astern), but you may sail any course you like. (Rule 12)

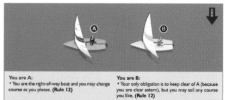

You are A:
• With B aiming to overtake you on your leeward side, you might be happy not to manoeuvre in case doing so discourages him, and he decides to take your wind on your windward side.
• On the other hand if you are approaching a port hand mark, you don't want him to get an inside overlap, so you may bear away to encourage him to stay to windward.
• While clear ahead, you remain the right-of-way boat and may luff or bear away as you please.

You are B:
• As you are clear astern you must keep clear; but you may luff or bear away as you please.

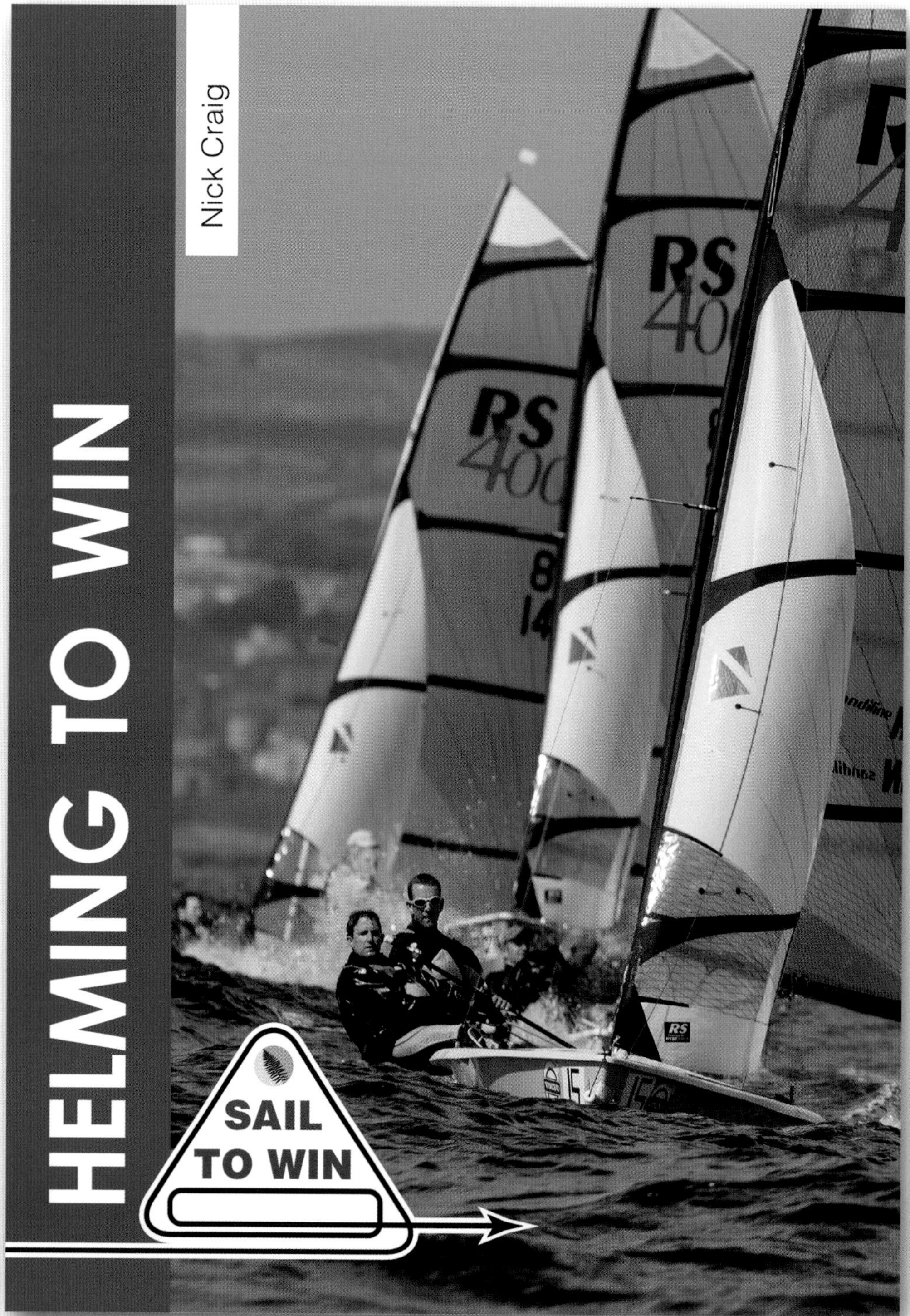
Nick Craig
HELMING TO WIN
SAIL TO WIN

Where to Look when Racing

When you first start sailing, or are new to a boat, you tend to look at your feet to ensure that you aren't tripping up. The key to progressing is looking further and further up and knowing when to switch between the modes.

Broadly, there are 5 modes (places to look):

1 **Your Feet** | **Jib / Main Telltales** 2 | 3 **The Water** | **Spotting Next Few Shifts** 4 | 5 **The Big Picture**

Mode 1: Your Feet

This is inevitable when you are new to the sport or a boat. It is an appropriate place to look when your boat handling is being pushed to its limit. Your boat handling limit will, of course, vary depending on how experienced you are in your chosen boat. However, you will miss a lot of windshifts and gusts if you look down too much.

You should move away from this mode as soon as possible, partly through being aware of where you are looking and by forcing yourself to look up. That can be hard as it may be outside your comfort zone and may mean that you fall over, or even out of the boat, occasionally, but it is a good thing to do at those training events.

Mode 2: Jib / Main Telltales

100% concentration on your telltales ensures that you are dead on the wind all of the time upwind and that your sails are always set optimally downwind. This is a good mode when boatspeed is critical, e.g. in a tight spot out of a start. However, you should eventually be able to keep your boat dead on the wind (or keep the sails optimally set) without spending much time staring at the telltales. Again, practice is key for this, forcing yourself to look at the water and not the jib is a good discipline.

Upwind Speed

The key reason why some people seem to be able to sail fast in any boat is good technique. Good technique means being able to sail a boat consistently flat and balanced as the wind changes in strength and direction with minimal use of the rudder. Often this is described as being 'in the groove'. Upwind speed is achieved by setting your boat up correctly and sailing it flat.

Getting 'In The Groove'

Sailing 'in the groove' is a wonderful feeling – you feel your boat sailing higher and faster than those around you.

Your boat is 'in the groove' when:
1. It is dead flat in all sea states.
2. Your foils are providing lift, as shown by slight weather helm (i.e. the boat tries to point to windward a touch when sailed flat).
3. Your sails are optimally set for the wind and wave conditions (which is a book in itself!).

Sailing Flat

Your boat needs to be sailed dead flat to be 'in the groove'. This is an unnatural position unless you have trained yourself to sail like this, because a few degrees of heel is more comfortable. An inclinometer (showing your angle of heel) is a

useful training aid, and it is also helpful to look behind at the ripples from the rudder to see that they are even. Sailing consistently flat is much harder than sailing flat momentarily. To do it consistently you need to be anticipating the heeling effect of gusts and lulls which can only be achieved by having your head out of the boat.

In training, and in training events, a good objective is to sail flat all of the time. This may slow you up at first because you may be focusing on this rather than your telltales, the next gust or the multitude of other things that sailors can be looking for. But be persistent and eventually sailing flat will become a habit which you don't need to concentrate on. It is then a lifetime skill which will give you a permanent edge over most sailors. Sailing consistently flat is the biggest jump in speed most sailors can make, and the cheapest way to increase boatspeed!

Sailing flat, not even slightly heeled, is the biggest jump in speed most sailors can make

---

Lots of body steering is required to stay on the waves

Sailing at Championships

As I have already said, sailing is a very complex sport. At training events, you should try to keep dissecting the sport, experimenting with new ideas, learning, putting your processes back together and then breaking them up again.

At big events you should keep it simple. Stop trying new things and sail instinctively. Most big events are won or lost before the event, so what you have learnt through the season will now show through. It is too late to change anything now, so this is the time to enjoy putting everything together and sail at your best without the distraction of training objectives!

By trying new things at the smaller events, the big events are in many ways easier, which is a nice mindset with which to go into a championship.

The best practice to get good at big fleet sailing is, unsurprisingly, big fleet sailing! Experienced big fleet sailors are able to glance around quickly and understand immediately where they are versus the fleet, understand how much risk they are taking and assess that against their objectives. This

sounds complex but with experience it becomes almost instinctive, so the sailor is focused on speed rather than having to look around at the fleet too much.

While a little tedious, checklists can be useful at big events as it is easy to forget something critical (e.g. food, the most important thing!). A checklist should include all the things you need, e.g. multitool, tape, spares, food, water, etc.

Being able to start well in big fleets is a key skill

COACH YOURSELF TO WIN

Jon Emmett

SAIL
TO WIN

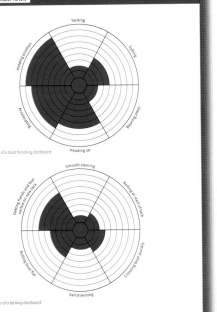

An example of a boat handling dartboard

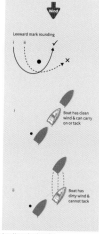

An example of a tacking dartboard

---

sorted before rounding the mark and give yourself a wide enough entrance to the mark to ensure a tight exit. In a perfect world, if a picture were taken just one boat length after the mark, you should not be able to tell that you have just rounded it. So whenever training always finish on a good leeward mark rounding, as it is such an important skill.

A good leeward mark rounding

Summary of Key Ideas

- Keep your wind clear or get into clean wind as soon as possible.
- Stay between the opposition and the next mark (directly upwind on the upwind legs, slightly offset on the downwind legs so as to have clean wind).
- Protect the favoured side of the course (the side with more wind, better current, etc.).

Advice from Olympic Gold Medallist (Laser class) Paul Goodison

❝ *I feel the key to tactics is being able to adapt quickly to changing situations. It is very much about weighing up the risk / reward for each action on the race course. Try to minimise risk and sail conservatively. Generally, the people who make the fewest mistakes win.*

It is important to be able to focus on the right thing at the right time. Different weather conditions and fleet positions will require different tactics. I try to keep things as simple as possible, and set myself small goals for different conditions. For example, in shifty conditions, I will always be on the lifted tack, sometimes even if this means that I am in dirty air. In stable conditions, I always make sure that I have clear wind. This may mean that I have to take a small header to clear my lane. I set out these goals for each day, as they are dependent on the conditions and stage of the regatta. It is easy to overcomplicate this area of sailing: generally the people that are winning are just keeping it simple. ❞

CHAPTER 2
Boat Handling

The phrase 'boat handling' refers to any skills that are not directly related to straight line speed. These can often be practised on land where the boat is securely tied to the trolley and you can analyse very carefully what is best to do with your hands and feet with no risk of a capsize.

The important thing is to be able to perform near perfect boat handling manoeuvres under pressure as this gives you lots of tactical options. For example, if you know that you can tack under someone without being rolled, or if you can gybe quickly making it hard for someone to cover you (or easier for you to cover them). You do so many tacks and gybes over the course of a race: if you can make each one just ½ boat length better, accumulatively that is a huge distance by the end of the series, and many fewer points at the end of a series.

It is also worth noting that slow speed boat handling skills, like those required pre-start, are very important too. It is not all about achieving rapid acceleration: being able to slow down, hold position and turn without going over a start line are all very important.

Practice

Practice makes perfect so, if you think of all the boat handling that you do during the course of a race, it is obvious that boat handling drills are an essential part of any campaign. When sailing high performance boats for the first time, just being able to get around the race course in the upper wind range can be a real achievement (and it is perhaps worth making sure that your first couple of sails are done in light to medium breezes!).

It is advisable to get your boat handling to a reasonable level before you hitch your boat up to go to your first open meeting as you cannot race effectively if your boat handling is not up to scratch (your strategy and tactics will be compromised if you cannot tack / gybe or get around the marks efficiently).

That old cliché: 'time on the water' is definitely true when it comes to perfecting boat handling, but remember that the more specific and demanding you make the exercises, the greater the potential improvement. By doing a good range of exercises (rather than simply going out and tacking and gybing) it is possible to keep motivation high, and old skills can soon be remembered again with intensive practice. In fact practising boat handling can be an excellent way of developing specific fitness (like doing fast spinnaker hoists and drops).

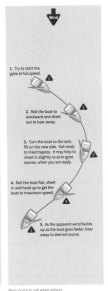

Wind

5. Roll the boat flat, head up to a close-hauled course and sheet in.

4. Roll the boat on top of you. Helm and crew move across the boat together, sheeting in as they reach the new side of the boat. Turn the boat onto a close reach on the new tack.

3. Keep the sails sheeted in until the bow goes past head to wind.

2. Sheet the mainsail in hard and move the boat towards the wind with minimum tiller movement.

1. Try to start the tack at full speed.

Best course to sail when tacking

Wind

1. Try to start the gybe at full speed.

2. Roll the boat to windward and sheet out to bear away.

3. Turn the boat so the sails fill on the new side. Get ready to hike/trapeze. It may help to sheet in slightly so as to gybe sooner, when you are ready.

4. Roll the boat flat, sheet in and head up to get the boat to maximum speed.

5. As the apparent wind builds up as the boat goes faster, bear away to desired course.

Best course to sail when gybing

TUNING TO WIN

Ian Pinnell

ANDREW
SIMPSON
SAILING
FOUNDATION

Bart

SAIL
TO WIN

What Each Control Does

You are now the proud owner of a boat, no doubt covered in multi-coloured control lines. Surely, you think, I don't need all this string?!

...I'm afraid you do. The ability to tune the rig ashore, and then tweak it afloat, is vital to your success.

This chapter looks at what each control does. I've divided it into two parts:
1. The standing rigging, spreaders, chocks and so on that you tend to set up ashore.
2. The control lines that you are constantly adjusting afloat, e.g. the vang, mainsheet, etc.

Standing Rigging

The Sails

When laid out on its own the sail is flat, with a curved luff

When set on a straight mast there is a belly in the sail

When the mast bends it takes out most of the belly

18

Control of the vertical angle of the jibsheet is achieved in three different ways, dependent on class.

1. Clewboard (e.g. 49er, 29er)
The sheet lead is constant on the deck and the angle of the jibsheet is altered by attaching it to a different hole on the clewboard. You may need to change hole if the mast rake alters.

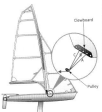

Clewboard

Pulley

2. Adjustable blocks (e.g. 505)

Adjustable blocks on jibsheet

3. Jib tracks (e.g. 2000)

Jib tracks

Whichever of the three methods is used, there should be sheeting lines marked on the jib so the crew can line up the jibsheet for the best angle.

A clewboard on a 29er

Sheeting lines marked on the jib

40

Step 4: Have A Look At The Mainsail

Pull up the mainsail and adjust the cunningham, outhaul and vang for light airs.

Sight up the mainsail, or lay a batten horizontally from the luff to the leech to show where the draft is. At mid-height the maximum draft should be ⅓ back from the mast. The diagram below shows what you're looking for.

Too little mast bend

Correct mast bend

Too much mast bend

Mainsail draft at mid-height

Open   Normal   Tight

Different leech tensions

Hounds

45%

Look from astern to see how open the leech is (above right).

With the cunningham slack, you should have creases running from the mast to a line from the hounds to 45% of the way along the boom. If the creases don't do this, adjust the spreaders, chocks and lowers until they do. **Speed creases are fast**, and it's definitely fastest if this whole triangle is filled with creases. (But do avoid the creases going more than 50% aft.)

With the cunningham slack you should have creases in this area

57

Step 6: Calibration

Calibrate all the control lines and record the settings you established in *Preparing Your Boat* Steps 1-5 and *The Initial Set-Up* Steps 1-5. For example, put a mark on the cascade vang system, and see how one of the blocks moves against this line.

P&B

Calibrate all your control lines & fittings and record the settings

Note that we have tuned for upwind. Don't worry about offwind tuning at this stage – you simply want the mainsail to be as full as possible downwind. Pre-bend, for example, doesn't come into it because the pre-bend is fore and aft. With the boom out you would need sideways pre-bend to affect the fullness!

59

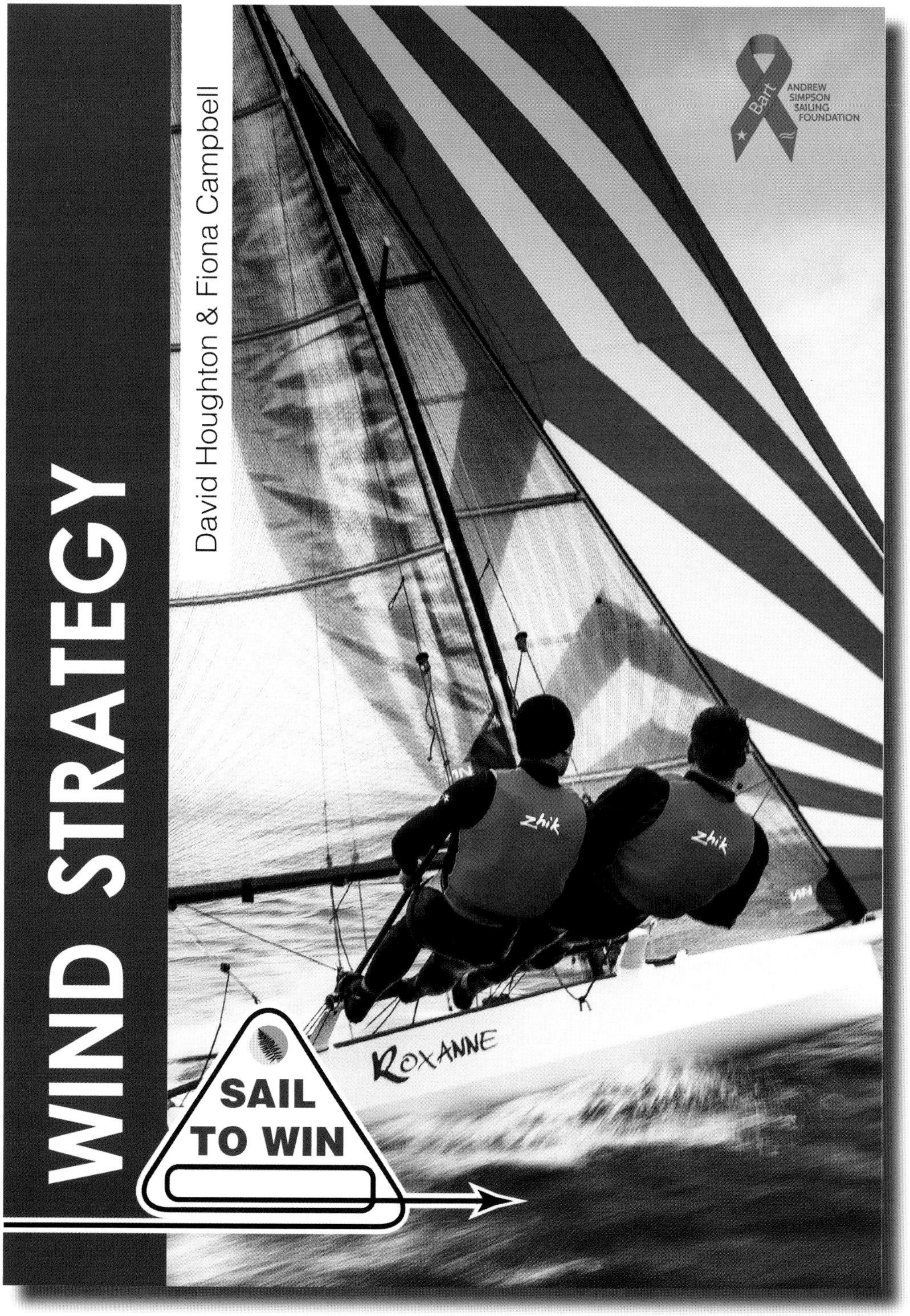

WIND STRATEGY

David Houghton & Fiona Campbell

ANDREW SIMPSON SAILING FOUNDATION

Bart

SAIL TO WIN

ROXANNE

zhik

CHAPTER 2
The Sailor's Wind

Anything moving requires energy to start it off, and in most cases to keep it going. The wind is no exception. Air moves around the Earth in response to heating by the sun. Equatorial regions receive the most heat, polar regions the least. The major wind systems of the world are all the result of heated air rising over equatorial regions and being replaced by colder air from polar regions. The zone where the major cold and warm winds meet is commonly known as the polar front, and is the birthplace of many of the larger weather systems – the depressions and anticyclones – of temperate latitudes.

The traditional (and easiest) way to map the movements of air around the world is to plot the values of pressure, or weight of air, at the Earth's surface. Such weather maps with their lines of equal pressure – isobars – have been in use for over a hundred years, ever since the invention of the electric telegraph. Weather satellites have provided pictorial evidence of the size, shape and main characteristics of depressions and anticyclones, the clouds acting as dye in the air to map out their development and decay.

A snippet of a weather map

In its simplest form: Heated air rises over the equator to be replaced by cooler air from the poles

Due to land and the Earth's rotation, this simple cell model (left) is modified (above)

CHAPTER 7
The Sea Breeze

The term 'sea breeze' is often used very loosely to denote any wind blowing onshore. But if we are to recognise, understand and use the changes in coastal winds which occur as the land warms, we need to be more precise and disciplined in our terminology. In what follows, the term 'sea breeze' is restricted to mean the wind which blows onshore when the warming of the land by the sun generates a closed circulation; the onshore breeze near the surface being supplied by air moving offshore in the same general area but higher up. This 'sea breeze' has very distinctive characteristics, which are predictable and usable. Distinguishing between it and other onshore winds is essential to answering the question 'which side will pay?'.

For the purposes of this chapter it is assumed that there is no gradient wind. While this may not be the case very often, it provides by far the easiest route to understanding the development and behaviour of the sea breeze throughout the world. In Chapter 8 we will see how the gradient wind encourages or inhibits the development of a sea breeze.

How It Starts
It is a sunny or bright day. The air over the land is warmed more than the air over the sea and the sea breeze mechanism begins to operate as follows:
1. The air over the land is warmed and expands. A rise of only 1 to 2°C above the sea temperature

is sufficient to start the sea breeze process. Hence the presence of a thin cover of cloud is unlikely to prevent a sea breeze.
2. This causes an excess of air (an imbalance of pressure) at some higher level, usually between 300 and 1,000 metres above sea level.
3. Air flows out seawards to remove the imbalance, helped by the offshore gradient wind.
4. Air moves downwards over the sea to replace that which is beginning to move onto the land.
5. This is the sea breeze.

It is worth noting that the time of start of the sea breeze is 'sun time' rather than 'clock time'.

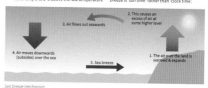

Sea breeze mechanism

CHAPTER 14
The Message Of The Clouds

Clouds tell of a wide variety of events in the atmosphere, some of them involving changes in the wind. Seen from a weather satellite orbiting thousands of kilometres above the Earth the clouds act as dye in the air, mapping out the large-scale weather systems. The depressions are particularly noticeable with their attendant troughs and fronts, but there is also a wide variety of smaller scale arrangements of clouds, some of them giving clues to the existence of wind patterns which, if they can be identified, will prove useful to the sailor.

Looked at from below, the clouds are just as meaningful but their message relates to events on a scale of a few hundred metres or so. Cumulus clouds, for instance, tell of pockets of rising air which are replaced by air moving downwards between the clouds. Occasionally there may be no wind except for the movement of air into a large cumulus cloud from all directions around it. In fact every cloud has a message of some sort, though not necessarily about the wind. The sailor needs to recognise features of the clouds which relate to the character of the wind – its gustiness for instance – or which foretell a change during the period of a race.

Many books on the weather concentrate attention on the major wind systems, the depressions and anticyclones, and a great deal is written about the clouds and changes in wind associated with their fronts, troughs and ridges. This information is of vital importance for anyone contemplating an ocean race; but a dinghy sailor about to compete for the next 1 or 2 hours on a small course is unlikely to be able to make much use of it.

Of one thing we are certain: knowledge of the clouds can help win races. And the more you practise observing the clouds, their evolution and associated wind patterns, the more impressive your performance will be. We will not say much here about high clouds – those above 3,000 metres

or so. Their message is normally about events far aloft or several hours ahead. We concentrate here on evidence of wind changes ranging from a couple of minutes to two or three hours ahead. But let us first consider a few simple observations which any layman might make and what we might deduce from them.

Cloud Colour
The colour of a cloud depends on how it is illuminated. If the sun is shining on it, it will appear white; if the sun is behind it, it will appear dark. If it is illuminated at a glancing angle when the sun is rising or setting, it will be beautifully coloured. This colour will change as the cloud moves or as the sun's elevation changes. The colour or change in colour of the cloud is of no consequence where the wind is concerned.

The colour of the cloud is irrelevant for the wind

CHAPTER 17
Water Currents

Very rarely is water absolutely still. It is normally moving in one direction or another for some reason, and any movement is important to the racing sailor. Only if the movement is uniform over the racing area and constant throughout the period of the race can it be discounted, since it does not benefit one helmsman over another. If the current changes across the course or during the race it may well be used to advantage.

For any particular place the pattern of ocean currents may be gleaned from the Admiralty Pilot for the area, and the tidal streams can be worked out from the appropriate tidal atlas or online. We want to consider here the variations from the data given in the tidal atlas or nautical almanac and show how to anticipate and recognise them.

Variations can occur for four main reasons:
- Interaction with the coast or islands.
- Variations in depth.
- The wind.
- Variations in temperature and salinity.

Interaction With The Coast Or Islands
You have only to stand on a river bank and watch the water flowing by to realise how easily eddies form in any bay or inlet, downstream from an obstruction or at the edge of a particularly fast part of the flow. Some of these eddies remain in the same place for long periods, others break away and are carried downstream by the main flow.

Spotting eddies at sea is often a matter of common sense coupled with observation. If a current is flowing past an obstacle, a bay or an inlet it is very likely that an eddy will form. The details of its shape and size, and whether or not it will break away from time to time, depend on the shape of the coastline and the depth of the water (right).

Eddies form downstream from an obstruction

Spotting eddies at sea

START TO FINISH

IN **GOOD COMPANY**

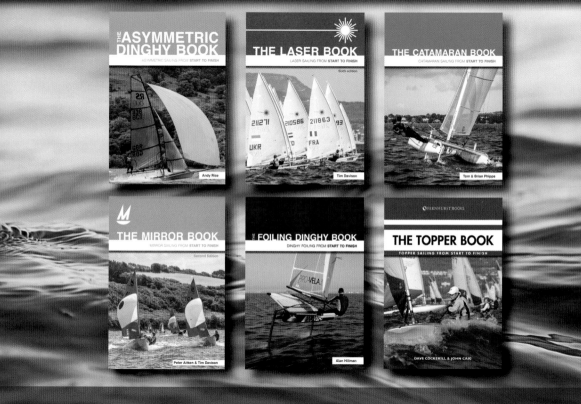

From beginner to serious racer, get the most out of your chosen vessel with the **Start to Finish** series.

Each book focusses on a different class or craft, designed to help sailors get started, develop skills and perform at the highest level.

Available in paperback and eBook from all good bookshops, websites and www.fernhurstbooks.com